Advance Prai   D0800781

The Gospel according

I'm amazed that nobody has really done this, not in this way. H. L. Hix, a first-rate poet and critic, has translated and edited the gospels with a deft hand, harmonizing the story in a way that brings the astonishing voice of Jesus to the fore. This is a brilliant piece of writing, make no mistake: a combination of Hix and the great gospel writers, whoever they were. I will gratefully keep this on my shelf beside the Bible.

—— Jay Parini, author of *Jesus: The Human Face of God*
and *The Way of Jesus*

Enjoy *The Gospel*, and discuss it with someone. To put it differently, just try to read this without imagining yourself in a discussion about it either among Biblical scholars (my first thought was that the Westar Institute, Sojourners, and the like ought consider this text), or people who are unsatisfied with church doctrines (I'm hosting a picnic next week), or clerical staff in a diocese that could use a little shaking up, or a book group that selects books that unsettle expectations. The Introduction delivers a most succinct and entertaining narration of the pragmatic ramifications of the legacy of the Gospels that made it into the Bible, and why it is most appropriate to resist the foregone conclusions that dominate contemporary expectations of what they are. If only Biblical studies as a field enjoyed such engaging clarity. Perhaps in addition to source, form and redaction criticism, we can now speak of Hix criticism.

Hix also argues for the value of his constructive wagers with refreshing brevity and boldness. He tells us he is doing what was done in the writing of the Biblical Gospels: He's writing a Gospel. *The Gospel*. His transparency with regard to the sources illuminates his remarkable breadth of knowledge pertinent to source and form criticism. Hix's mastery and obvious delight in weaving a narrative arc by drawing from forty-eight additional sources to the Biblical Gospels, an arc that begins with the birth of Mary and concludes with the resurrection, elevates the reading to a kind of artistry that specialists will particularly enjoy. May *Thunder: Perfect Mind* find xerself (see below) appearing again and again on our contemporary climate crisis landscapes.

Three particularly relevant strategies that Hix uses include: staying true to simple Greek words rather than translating them with specialized English words, and in light of this first effort, he translates an immanent xe (see next item) in the sky we know rather than a transcendent God in heaven that we cannot know, and finally he "tilts" gender. Biblical scholarship has been described up to this point as offering three paths: progressive feminist (such as Mary Daly's *Wickedary*), gender neutral (avoid pronouns at all cost) or retention of He, Father, and Son, claiming Biblical inerrancy. Hix delivers another alternative with the introduction of fother (mother + father), and perhaps with a nod to Generation X or Z, the xon of humanity replaces the Son of Man, and the pronouns he, him, and his become xe, xer, and xers (where the x is pronounced as zh). These three very serious forms of strategic play transform the reading and thus reflection on The Gospel. This book should be entertained by people interested in the enduring power of Biblical narratives. It should be discussed by people who want to challenge the theological, class and gender hierarchies of Christian doctrine and institutions. And those interested in the audacity of *The Gospel* as it challenges and transforms narrative will find herein a worthy jest for serious contemplation.

— Mary L. Keller, Westar Fellow and author
of the forthcoming *Spirit of Climate Change*

THE GOSPEL

Also by H. L. Hix

POETRY
Rain Inscription
American Anger
I'm Here to Learn to Dream in Your Language
As Much As, If Not More Than
First Fire, Then Birds
Incident Light
Legible Heavens
God Bless
Chromatic
Shadows of Houses
Surely As Birds Fly
Rational Numbers
Perfect Hell

TRANSLATIONS
Jüri Talvet, *Yet, Love, Illumine Us*, trans. with the author
Tautvyda Marcinkevičiūtė, *Terribly in Love: Selected Poems*, ed. with Julie Kane
Juhan Liiv, *Snow Drifts, I Sing: Selected Poems*, trans. with Jüri Talvet
Eugenijus Ališanka, *from unwritten histories*, trans. with the author
Jüri Talvet, *Of Snow, of Soul: New Selected Poems*, trans. with the author
Jüri Talvet, *Estonian Elegy: Selected Poems*, trans. with the author
Juhan Liiv, *The Mind Would Bear No Better*, trans. with Jüri Talvet
On the Way Home: An Anthology of Contemporary Estonian Poetry, trans. with Jüri Talvet
Jüri Talvet, *A Call for Cultural Symbiosis*, trans. with the author
Eugenijus Ališanka, *City of Ash*, trans. with the author

ANTHOLOGIES
Counterclaims: Poets and Poetries, Talking Back
Uncoverage: Asking After Recent Poetry
There's This Place I Know...
Ley Lines
Made Priceless: A Few Things Money Can't Buy
New Voices: Contemporary Poetry from the United States
Wild and Whirling Words: A Poetic Conversation

THEORY AND CRITICISM
Demonstrategy: Poetry, For and Against
Lines of Inquiry
As Easy As Lying: Essays on Poetry
Understanding William H. Gass
Understanding W. S. Merwin
Spirits Hovering Over the Ashes: Legacies of Postmodern Theory
Morte d'Author: An Autopsy

THE GOSPEL

✝

ACCORDING TO

H. L. HIX

Broadstone

Library of Congress Control No. 2020946803

ISBN 978-1-937968-74-8

Design & Typesetting by Larry W. Moore.
Cover Design by Stephanie Potter &
the author.
Cover art by Piper Shepard,
"Iris 3:1," 2013, 25"x25"x1.5",
digitally printed cotton,
corsage pins on drywall.
Reproduced by permission of the artist.

Broadstone Books
An Imprint of
Broadstone Media LLC
418 Ann Street
Frankfort, KY 40601-1929
BroadstoneBooks.com

CONTENTS

About This Book   ix

The Gospel   3

Additional Reading   151

ABOUT THIS BOOK

In the centuries since humans began building permanent dwellings, many hundreds of houses have been built facing waterfalls. Not until 1935, though, did anyone test what happens if in building a home we don't assume that a view of the falls means a view from a location level with the falls and across from them. The result was Frank Lloyd Wright's Fallingwater, one proof that from a different vantage point (in this case *over* the falls instead of *facing* them) things might look very different.

In the centuries since Gutenberg invented the printing press, many millions of copies of gospels have been printed. Not until now, though, has anyone tested what happens if we don't assume the primacy of the four gospels sanctioned by the Church. Even books about other gospels and editions of other gospels defer to the institutional canon by qualifying other gospels as, for instance, *gnostic* gospels or *apocryphal* gospels.

Fallingwater resulted from asking what the waterfall looks like from a different vantage: What if we look from atop the waterfall instead of alongside it? *The Gospel* resulted from asking what the gospel looks like from a different vantage: What if we give attention equally to canonical and noncanonical gospels? What if we do not keep existing gospels apart, reading them always and only separately, but integrate them instead into a single narrative? What if we foreground universality in God and Jesus by referring to them without gender specification? What if we don't grant that, just because we've always used certain words in English translations, they are the best or only match for the words used in the original? By posing such questions as these, *The Gospel* takes a vantage point never taken before, one from which things look very different.

The difference between *The Gospel* and the Church-enforced four is not total; it is not *opposition*. *The Gospel* offers familiar miracles (turning water into wine), familiar episodes (Jesus walking on water), familiar sayings ("Do unto others…"), familiar parables (the good Samaritan), and familiar assertions ("Where two or three are gathered…"). The difference is, though, substantial. Alongside such familiar elements, *The Gospel* offers less familiar miracles (five-year-old Jesus raising from the dead a playmate who has fallen from a rooftop), less familiar episodes (a doubting midwife's hand withering when she checks Mary's private parts to confirm virginity), less familiar sayings ("The god is a human-eater…"), less familiar parables (the householder who feeds the right food to each animal), and less familiar assertions ("I am nearer you than the clothes on your body").

The difference is substantial enough to warrant this introductory note which, like the legend on a map (solid lines stand for paved roads, dashed lines for dirt trails; 1 inch = 1 mile), tries to give, not an interpretation, but just enough description and context to clarify: a succinct "here's what you're looking at."

To describe what this book *is*, it helps to declare what it is *not*:

• It is not a scholarly monograph *about* the four Gospels. Composing *The Gospel* demanded a great deal of research, but the book is not a presentation of that research *per se*, in the form of an argument, after the manner of, say, Matthew Larsen's *Gospels Before the Book*. It does not consist in my writings about ancient texts, but in the ancient texts themselves.

• This book is not a commentary *on* the four Gospels, on the order of, say, Muddiman and Barton's *The Gospels* in the Oxford Bible Commentary series. Although I hope it adds perspective, its purpose is not primarily to add information. Again, *The Gospel* is not my words *about* the words of Gospel writers, but the words of Gospel writers themselves.

• This book is not a devotional guide *to* the four Gospels, as, say, the Foursquare Church's *Journey Through the Gospels* is, intended to help a reader secure spiritual instruction or value from a reading of the four Gospels. This book is not advice on how to secure gospel from a Gospel, but a Gospel from which one might seek to secure gospel.

• *The Gospel* is not a fictionalization *of* the four Gospels, in the way that many novels and films reimagine gospel narratives: Nikos Kazantzakis' novel *The Last Temptation of Christ*, say, or the Martin Scorsese film made from it; Mel Gibson's film *The Passion of the Christ*; the novels *The Gospel according to Jesus Christ* and *The Childhood of*

Jesus by Nobel Prize winners José Saramago and J. M. Coetzee, respectively; and so on. This book is not "creative writing" or "imaginative literature" in the sense that applies to those works. I did not "make up" anything here. I selected, arranged, and translated all the material, but I invented none of it: everything in *The Gospel* derives from ancient sources, nothing originates with me.

This book *is* an account of the life and teachings of Jesus, composed by gathering many ancient sources (including but not at all limited to the four Gospels), selecting material from those sources, translating the selected material into English, and synthesizing the selected material into a single narrative.

One clarification of *why* such an account is called for comes from a musical analogy. Any of several gestures might accompany my declaration that "I've got 'the Moonlight Sonata' right here in my hands!" I might hold up my copy of the printed score, or I might hold up my vintage Vladimir Horowitz vinyl, or I might hold up my hands themselves. In each case, my conversation partner would know what I meant, though in each case I would mean something slightly different, and in each case, the Moonlight Sonata I held in my hands both would and would not be the Moonlight Sonata itself. For instance, the score I hold up is the Moonlight Sonata: it's not "Rhapsody in Blue" or *Pride and Prejudice* or a turnip. But the score I hold up is not the Moonlight Sonata: it's *the score* of the Moonlight Sonata. We have ways to point to the gap. When I read the score of the Moonlight Sonata, I read for the Moonlight Sonata. When I listen to my Vladimir Horowitz recording of the Moonlight Sonata, I listen for the Moonlight Sonata. When I show off for drunken friends as a cocktail party winds down, I impose on them *a performance* of the Moonlight Sonata. When one of those friends complains to another about how poorly I played, she might say, "*That* wasn't the Moonlight Sonata."

An analogous gap faces readers of any written work (the paperback on my nightstand is a copy of *Middlemarch*, not *Middlemarch* itself), and certainly faces readers of the gospel. In reading a Gospel (whatever copy I have of whatever Gospel, say my New Revised Standard Version of the Gospel According to Luke in a 2007 printing of an Oxford edition), I read for the gospel (for what it is that Luke's account is an account *of*). There are many ways to describe the gap: the scholar Mieke Bal, for instance, distinguishes text (Luke's written Gospel) from story (how Luke told things) from fabula (what Luke was telling); I myself have distinguished ore (the events and sayings of Jesus), arché (Jesus himself), archive (what Luke seeks to convey), artisan (Luke), artifact (the text of the book attributed to Luke). However the difference is parsed, I read words on a page in order to grasp something those words convey. The gap has sometimes been signaled by the typographical convention of capitalization: "Gospel" to refer to a written account, "gospel" to refer to what the written account is an account of. Even if I hold "the four Gospels" sacred, the gap still applies: I read the Gospel of Luke to receive from it the gospel.

In the context of that broad problematic, various concerns arise about the customary presentation of those vehicles of gospel, "the four Gospels." *The Gospel* was composed in response to the following concerns.

1. Source Bottleneck: The very term "the four Gospels" indicates how successfully history has identified the gospel with four particular Gospels, those of Matthew, Mark, Luke, and John. The success of that identification is not confined within the Church. To give just one example, the dictionary that came pre-loaded on my laptop gives three definitions of the word *gospel*, but supplements one of the three with this passage, highlighted by a shaded text box: "The four Gospels ascribed to St. Matthew, St. Mark, St. Luke, and St. John all give an account of the ministry, crucifixion, and resurrection of Christ, although the Gospel of John differs greatly from the other three. There are also several later, apocryphal accounts that are recorded as Gospels." The dictionary purports to be a neutral, "objective" source of information, not one advancing a viewpoint specific to the Church, yet by saying that the accounts of Matthew, Mark, Luke, and John are Gospels and that all other accounts are *recorded as* Gospels, it directly implies the authenticity of the accounts of Matthew, Mark, Luke, and John, and the inauthenticity of other accounts. Its way of delivering the truth that there are several later accounts implies the falsehood that there are *only* later accounts, not also earlier ones. And its characterization of the later accounts as apocryphal makes it sound as though apocryphal-ness were inherent in the accounts themselves (the way, say, oddness is inherent in the numbers 1, 3, 5, 7, and so on), rather than being a way of categorizing accounts (as a cheese plate's being an "appetizer" or a "dessert" has to do with how we categorize it).

The identification of the gospel with the four Gospels has been so successful that many persons are unaware that any other Gospels have been written. By its ambiguity, the term "the four Gospels" invites a conflation of the factual *truth* that Matthew, Mark, Luke, and John are the only four Gospels that the Christian Church sanctions as sacred scripture, the *judgment* that Matthew, Mark, Luke, and John are the only four Gospels that convey the gospel, and the *falsehood* that Matthew, Mark, Luke, and John are the only four Gospels that exist.

As a way of resisting that conflation, *The Gospel* veers away from "source bottleneck," the customary presentation of *only* the four Gospels, by drawing on many sources. Substantial selections do come from Matthew, Mark, Luke, and John, but substantial portions do not. Here is a complete list, in order of first appearance, of the other sources from which at least one passage comes:

> *Melchizedek*
> *The Concept of Our Great Power*
> *The Gospel of Thomas*
> *The Gospel of Truth*
> *The Prayer of Paul*
> *The Gospel of Pseudo-Matthew*
> *The Proto-Gospel of James*
> *Trimorphic Protennoia*
> *The Infancy Gospel of Thomas*
> *Tripartite Tractate*
> *The Gospel of Philip*
> *The Gospel according to the Egyptians*
> *The Dialogue of the Savior*
> *The Odes of Solomon*
> *Psalms of Heracleides*
> *The Treatise on the Resurrection*

The Apocryphon of James
The Acts of Peter
The Interpretation of Knowledge
Authoritative Discourse
The Book of Thomas the Contender
The Wisdom of Jesus Christ
Naassene Hymn
Epistula Apostolorum
Origen
The Gospel according to the Hebrews
Second Discourse of the Great Seth
The Apocryphon of John
Symeon of Mesopotamia
Papyrus Egerton 2
Justin
Pseudo-Cyprian
Papias
The Concept of Our Great Power
Papyrus Oxyrhynchus 840
The Teachings of Silvanus
The Second Revelation of James
The Testimony of Truth
Thunder: Perfect Mind
Pseudo-Clement
The Acts of John
The Gospel of Judas
The Gospel of Nicodemus
The Report of Pontius Pilate
The Gospel according to Mary
The Letter of Peter to Philip
The Revelation of Peter
Manichaean Psalms of the Bema

In some cases, selections incorporated into *The Gospel* are arranged by "lining them up," as when Luke's account of the circumcision and presentation of the baby Jesus is followed by a passage of praise from Trimorphic Protennoia. In other cases, selections are arranged by "interweaving them," as when a sentence from the Gospel of Thomas and a sentence from the Gospel of Philip are inserted into the Beatitudes as they appear in the Gospel of Matthew.

2. Enforced Separation: The four Gospels consistently get presented in a certain way. That way includes a certain sequence: we know them as Matthew, Mark, Luke, and John; it sounds "wrong" to say Mark, John, Matthew, and Luke. Even more basic than sequence, though, is separation: they can be consistently presented in that sequence because they are consistently kept separate from one another. Over and over, Gospels have been put side-by-side; *The Gospel* puts them *together*. Surely there is value in presenting, say, the four canonical Gospels, each in its entirety, one by one, but it is severely limiting to present them *always* and *only* in that way. Side-by-side presentation results in fragmentation: for example, Matthew tells about an angel's alerting *Joseph* that Jesus will be born; Luke tells about an angel's alerting *Mary* that Jesus will be born; and Mark tells us nothing about either alert. Side-by-side presentation results also in repetition: for example, Matthew, Mark, and Luke all three tell the parable of the sower, practically word-for-word. Countless editions *juxtapose* the canonical Gospels; until now, not a single one *integrates* them, much less does so with additional sources also integrated, and on equal terms.

Disrupting enforced separation has major consequences. For example, by selecting four Gospels and mandating a mode of presentation (separately, in a sequence, with Matthew first), institutional history plants the Gospels firmly in patriarchy: Matthew's Gospel begins with a patriarchal genealogy, so Jesus' identity is introduced to readers by a list of five women and forty-two men. By altering what is presented, and in what order, *The Gospel* alters the relation of the gospel to a pervasive social construct: instead of beginning with an entrenchment in patriarchy, it begins with an homage to the power of life.

The Gospel is not broken into the sort of numbered or titled chapters typical of a novel or memoir, but instead into segments within a continuous narrative ordered chronologically from birth through childhood then adulthood then death. This "outline" gives a highlight or two from each segment, to give an at-a-glance overview of the whole:

- Introduction.
- Invocation.
- Birth and childhood of Mary; birth of John; betrothal of Mary and Joseph.
- Birth of Jesus; presentation at the Temple.
- Flight from King Herod; return from Egypt.
- Episodes from Jesus' childhood.
- Baptism by John; temptation in the wilderness.
- Marriage at Cana; woman at the well.
- Herod kills John; Jesus' first preaching.
- Healing the ruler's son.
- Sermon on the mount.
- Bread from the sky.
- Healing the centurion's slave; stilling the storm; Gerasene demoniac.
- Healing a paralyzed person; healing the woman with a hemorrhage.
- Sending of the twelve; I've come to bring not peace but a sword; ministering women.
- Parable of the sower.
- Feeding of the 5,000; walking on water.
- The transfiguration; healing a boy with epilepsy.
- Parable of the lost sheep; parable of the unmerciful servant.
- Parable of the good Samaritan; parable of the prodigal son.
- My time has not yet come.
- Healing the bent woman; parable of the rich man and Lazarus.
- Parable of the laborers in the vineyard; healing of Bartimeus; story of Zacchaeus.
- Entry into Jerusalem; the withered fig tree.
- About paying tribute to Caesar; the greatest commandment; the widow's gift.
- The woman caught in adultery; I am from above.
- Parable of the ten maidens; prediction of the last judgment.
- Healing of the blind man; the good shepherd.

• Light and darkness; the raising of Lazarus.
• Judas' mystical vision.
• The last supper; Satan enters Judas; love one another.
• Jesus arrested, tried, and sentenced.
• The crucifixion, burial, and resurrection.
• Appearances and teachings after the resurrection; doubting Thomas.
• Much else could be written.
• Benediction.

The structure of the book is determined by the selection and sequencing of source passages, at the large scale of that outline, but also within each of those segments. A few segments come entirely from one source, but most combine material from more than one source. Here is a representative sequence of five passages, from the approximately 450 that compose the book. This sequence occurs within the ninth segment, the one that includes Jesus' first preaching.

Luke 4:16-21	Rejection at Nazareth 1
Dialogue of the Savior 130:14-22	Streams of honey
Odes of Solomon 42	Overcoming death
Mark 6:2-4	Rejection at Nazareth 2
Gospel of Thomas 105	sonofabitch

The Gospel of Luke is a canonical Gospel, written in Greek. The Dialogue of the Savior is a second-century Gospel in Coptic, preserved in a codex in the Nag Hammadi library. The Odes of Solomon are hymns in Syriac, possibly second-century. The Gospel of Mark is a canonical Gospel, in Greek. The Gospel of Thomas is a noncanonical Gospel, in Coptic. *The Gospel* integrates its components without distinguishing canonical from noncanonical, and without marking transitions from one source to another.

3. Example Blindness: Another motivation for composing *The Gospel* was to contest a historically entrenched proscription. Under the influence of the Christian Church, it has come to be acceptable to *read* what the writers of the canonical Gospels *wrote*, but unacceptable to *do* what they *did*. The Gospel writers did not sit down at a blank page and record from memory their personal experiences. The writer of Luke, for instance, narrates a conversation in which an angel informs Mary that she will give birth to a child who will inherit the throne of David and rule forever, but Luke wasn't there for that conversation, any more than the writer of John was there "in the beginning" when "the Word was with God." The Gospel writers drew on the sources available to them, synthesizing from those sources an account they considered relevant and timely. The mode of regard sanctioned instutionally is to take as authoritative and final those accounts themselves. *The Gospel* arises from a different mode of regard: not taking as final the four canonical Gospel accounts, but taking as valuable the methodology that generated them. I have tried, that is to say, to imitate the process undertaken by the writers of the Biblical Gospels, fulfilling their example by assembling the sources available to me and synthesizing from them an account I take to be relevant and timely. Those available sources include the Biblical Gospels themselves, but even that is consistent with their precedent: the Gospel according to Mark was one of the sources for the writers of the Gospels according to Matthew and Luke.

Resistance to example blindness is not unrelated to resistance to source bottleneck and enforced separation. The writers of ancient Gospels wrote by hand, and had only handwritten sources: there were vastly fewer copies available of any source. Today, there are millions of copies of the four Gospels in print, never mind their availability on line. Even sources far less well-known are available to any reader with access to a library. Any reader of this book has nearly instant access to any of the dozens of sources used in composing *The Gospel*. Which is to say that one who follows the example of earlier Gospel writers in drawing on available sources has many more sources to draw on than they did. That situation is more exaggerated today than it was even one hundred years ago, since several of the sources drawn on in composing *The Gospel* are from the Nag Hammadi Library, which was (re)discovered in 1945, and not available to scholars until the early 1970s.

The sources on which *The Gospel* draws (enumerated above) all are readily available, each published in at least one book, and some in numerous books. Some of the particular books in which I found them are noted below, in the "Additional Reading" section. My process, my attempt to overcome example blindness, involved several steps: accumulation, internalization, selection, arrangement, and translation. Which draws attention to another of the concerns that motivates *The Gospel*.

4. Translation Inertia: By "translation inertia" I mean the tendency, strongest in often-translated and widely-read texts, and thus very strong in the four Gospels, to replicate in later translations word choices from earlier translations because they are now familiar, rather than because they are still apt. For many words in the original language, one English translation has come to be taken for granted, despite being inaccurate or misleading. *The Gospel* actively resists such translation inertia. The issue of translation inertia arises not only in relation to the canonical Gospels, which have been translated often enough for there to *be* customary translations, but also in relation to the other sources on which *The Gospel* draws: even though the non-canonical sources have not been translated as often, they still use words that are used in the canonical Gospels, so translations of them still face the problem of translation inertia. Here are a few examples, with very brief rationales, to illustrate the fresh look *The Gospel* attempts to offer in resistance to translation inertia.

> Existing versions of the Biblical Gospels all translate the Greek *kurios* (κύριος) as "Lord." This had a certain resonance in King James England, where "Lord" was a title in current use, but a contemporary U.S. citizen has no daily-life reference point for a "lord." Yet to the original audience of the Greek Gospels, there *was* a sense of the word *kurios* that preceded its application to Jesus. For example, the same word is also applied to Pilate, and to the householder in the parable of the laborers in the vineyard: they are called *kurios* just like Jesus is. *The Gospel* translates *kurios* not as "Lord" but as "boss," as for example at Matthew 9:28: where other translations have two blind persons respond to a question from Jesus with "Yea, Lord" or "Yes, Lord," *The Gospel* has them respond with "Yes, boss." Instead of giving a narrowly

specialized English word for a common Greek word with a wide range of reference, *The Gospel* replaces the common Greek word with a common English one.

The Greek word *ouranos* (οὐρᾰνός) offers a different kind of example. Prior English translations, following the King James Version, repeat a consistent pattern in using two different words to translate *ouranos*, "air" when it is used in connection with birds and "heaven" when it is used in connection with God. Although that distinction conveys the range of meaning of *ouranos*, it also creates a profoundly misleading impression. A reader of any prior English translation of Matthew 6:26, such as the New Revised Standard Version's "Look at the birds of the air; they neither sow nor reap nor gather into barns, and yet your heavenly Father feeds them," would think that the birds are in one place, the air, and God is in another place, heaven. But that is not what Matthew says. The Greek uses the same word, *ouranos*, to designate the medium with which the birds and God are associated. They are the birds of the *ouranos*, and he is your *ouranos*-ly Father. The primary meaning of the Greek word is the region in which birds fly; only secondarily, by extension, does it refer to a realm, figuratively above us, in which deities may reside. In English, though, "heaven" refers primarily to the figuratively "up" realm of deities, and only derivatively to the region in which birds fly. So, instead of separating God and the birds, as prior English translations do, placing God in "heaven" and birds in "the air," *The Gospel* chooses the English word with the same primary meaning as the Greek word, and places birds and God both in the "sky." Thus Matthew 6:26 becomes "Look to the birds in the sky that don't plant or harvest or gather into barns, yet your father in the sky feeds them." In *The Gospel*, God is not *above* the environment birds live in, but *within* that environment. As with resistance to source bottleneck, enforced separation, and example blindness, resistance to translation inertia has consequences. In all prior English translations of the Biblical Gospels, God is stationed outside the earth's atmosphere; *The Gospel* restores the original sense of the Greek, which locates God *within* the biosphere.

The Greek word *angelos* (ἄγγελος) is, perhaps obviously, the source of the English word angel, so other English versions translate *angelos* as "angel." But *angelos*, like *kurios*, was a common Greek word, not a specialized religious word, as the English *angel* is. The English *angel* calls up images of white-robed figures with wings and haloes, but the Greek word meant anyone (most typically a normal, mortal, earthly human) sent with a message from one person to another. (The Greek word had corresponding forms: the verb *angello* (ἀγγέλλω) meant to carry a message, the noun *angelia* (ἀγγελία) was the message itself. The Greek word translated "gospel" was *euangelion* (εὐαγγέλιον), meaning a good message.) Instead of "angel," then, I have translated *angelos* as "emissary," to restore the original sense of someone sent with a message. So, in contrast to the New American Bible's translation of Matthew 28:5 as "Then the angel said to the women in reply, 'Do not be afraid!...'," *The Gospel* translates the same passage as "In response, the emissary said to the women, Don't fear."

Similarly, the Greek *daimon* (δαίμων) is usually translated by the English word that comes from it, *demon*. The English "demon," though, carries a connotation of evil: demons are always and essentially evil. The Greek *daimon*, though, might be good or evil. The *daimonion* that, in Plato's *Apology*, Socrates says helps him avoid making mistakes, for example, is very good. That range of moral states makes it sensible to qualify what kind of *daimon* is being observed, as occurs in Luke 4:33, translated in the New American Standard Bible as "And there was a man in the synagogue possessed by the spirit of an unclean demon...." In English, the "unclean" is redundant, since all demons are unclean. To push back against the misconception conveyed by translating *daimon* with "demon," *The Gospel* translates it with the morally neutral term "visitant." This allows the qualification in Luke 4:33 to add meaning, not simply to be redundant: "In the synagogue one man, held by the breath of a toxic visitant...."

Instead of the usual translation "spirit" for the Greek *pneuma* (πνεῦμα), *The Gospel* translates it as "breath." Instead of the usual translation "sin" for the Greek *hamartia* (ἁμαρτία), *The Gospel* translates it as "error." Instead of the usual translation "Christ" for the Greek *christos* (χριστός), *The Gospel* translates it as "salve." Instead of the usual translation "disciple" for the Greek *mathetes* (μἄθητής), *The Gospel* translates it as "apprentice." Instead of the usual translation "repent" for the Greek *metanoeo* (μετανοέω), *The Gospel* translates it as "reconsider." Instead of the usual "resurrection" for the Greek *anastasis* (ἀνάστασις), *The Gospel* translates it as "standing up." And so on, for numerous recurring words.

I am under no illusions about these and similar choices in translation: no translation can possibly reproduce the original perfectly. I have tried, though, to resist translation inertia by applying the general rule of *not* replacing non-specialized Greek words with specialized English words. If an English word has come to be used exclusively or primarily in religious contexts, I have sought an alternative when translating Greek (or Latin or Coptic) words that were not exclusively or primarily used in religious contexts.

5. Gender Tilt: One instance of resisting translation inertia in *The Gospel* is so pervasive that it merits mention on its own. It differs from the examples just given, in seeking not to *restore* a feature of the original language but to *overcome* a feature that the original languages and English share. In Greek, Latin, and Coptic, as traditionally in English, God is referred to as male: a father, not a mother; a he, not a she. This makes gospel universalism harder to convey in regard to gender than in regard to ethnicity or nationality. It is easy to make divine favor available to all persons if the Jews are God's chosen people because God *chose* the Jews, not because God *is* Jewish, but it is hard to make divine favor available to all persons if God — God *himself* — is male, possessed of xy chromosomes, testicles, and a beard.

The cognitive dissonance of portraying as male a purportedly universal deity and protagonist has been sustained, rather than reduced, as translations have continued to replicate in English the gendering of God and Jesus in the originals. It is easy to see why translations have done so, since the gendering is embedded in the relevant languages themselves. But by a few coinages, by *changing* the language, *The Gospel* sidesteps that problem. Where God is referred to in the source texts as a father, *The Gospel*, merging the words "father" and "mother," uses "fother," so, for example, instead of declaring that "I and the father are one," in *The Gospel* Jesus declares that "I and the fother are one." Where Jesus is referred to as a son, *The Gospel* uses "xon," so for example in the annunciation Mary is told not that she will bear a son but that she will bear a xon. (Pronouncing it "zun" allows for an aural as well as a visual difference from "son.") When referring to Jesus or God, substitutes are used for gendered pronouns: "he" becomes "xe," "him" becomes "xer," and "his" becomes "xer" or "xers" as appropriate. So for example, what the New Revised Standard Version translates as "he will reign over the house of Jacob forever; his kingdom will never end," *The Gospel* translates as "across the ages xe will rule the house of Jacob, and to xer reign there will be no end." (Pronouncing the pronouns as "zhe," "zher," and "zhers" allows for aural distinction from "she," so that *xe* neither looks like *he* nor sounds like *she*.) These measures sometimes combine with other gender-muting measures, so for example the formula usually translated "the Son of Man" is translated in *The Gospel* as "the xon of humanity." They also resonate with gender-saturated moments, such as Matthew 19:10-12, which in *The Gospel* becomes the first instance of Jesus speaking explicitly on behalf of the genderqueer. Because gendered forms of identification and reference occur so frequently, this revision of those forms influences every page, and nearly every sentence, of *The Gospel*.

In addressing those five concerns, *The Gospel* defies the institutional history that admits only four Gospels, keeps them separate from one another, treats them as objects rather than examples, translates them narrowly, and perpetuates their gender hierarchization. That institutional history is strong, and has been rigidly enforced, but in defying it *The Gospel* seeks to clear away obstructions between Gospel and gospel. The Gospel seeks, that is, to refresh what it might mean to pursue the ideal to which the poet Czeslaw Milosz gives eloquent expression: "it is proper that we move our finger / Along letters more enduring than those carved in stone."

THE GOSPEL

I attest here to the habitation of xe who is among and within we who would be.

In the age of the soul will come the human who knows the great power. Xe will receive it and know it. Xe will be sustained by the mother's milk. Speaking in parables, xe will proclaim the age to come, as xe spoke to Noah in the age of the flesh. With every word xe uttered, xe spoke in seventy-two languages. With xer words, xe opened the gates of the skies. Xe humiliated the overseer of the underworld, ending his rule by raising the dead.

Then, in a great imbroglio, the principals directed their wrath against xer, wanting to offer xer to the overseer of the underworld. They knew the one of xer apprentices whose soul smoldered, and xe handed over to them the one they didn't know. Intent, they seized xer, they transferred xer to the overseer of the underworld, but xe prepared xerself, and humiliated them.

The overseer of the underworld found xer flesh such that it could not be held and displayed to the principals. He kept protesting, Who is this? What is xe? Xer word has abolished the law of the age, xe is from the word of the power of life.

Xe defeated the authority of the principals, who could not control xer. The principals tried to figure out what had just happened, but didn't recognize this as the sign of their demise, and the changing of the age. The sun set at midday, and the day went dark. The visitants were disturbed. After this xe will be seen ascending. The sign of the coming age will appear, and ages themselves will dissolve.

The self-deceiving will say of xer that xe was not born, though xe was born, that xe did not eat, though xe did eat, that xe did not drink, though xe did drink, that xer flesh was not flesh, though it was flesh, that xe did not suffer and die, though xe did suffer and xe did die, that xe did not rise from the dead, though xe did rise from the dead. But those who embrace truth will be embraced by hope and life.

Those who understand what is presented here will become graceful. They will be graceful because they understand truth. Those who have followed xer, who have labored in their homelands, will find rest in the skies. They will journey, repeating xer words at will.

But look, everything that is to be has happened already.

At the origin was the word, and the word was of the god, and god was the word. At the origin it was of the god. All began through it, and without it nothing that did begin began. In it was life, and the life was the light of humans. The light shines through the darkness, and the darkness cannot contain it. Humans, seeing images, see by the light but don't see the light they see by. Humans see the lit, not the light.

This is the gospel of the sought that seekers seek, the completion given by the fother's mercy. Through the hidden mystery Jesus the salve enlightened those who were in the darkness of forgetting. Xer light revealed as a path the truth xe taught. Xe teaches those willing to be taught, the living written in the book of the living. Those willing to be taught are taught about themselves, by the fother to whom the teaching turns them.

I invoke you who are now as you always already were in the name beyond all naming, through Jesus the salve, the boss of bosses, officer of timelessnesses. Give me of your irrevocable gifts through the xon of humanity, the breath, the advocate of truth. Give me authority, I ask of you. Give me healing for my body, I ask it through the source of good news, and recover my soul and my breath to lasting light. Reveal to my mind the firstborn of the fullness of grace. Grant what no emissary's eyes have seen, what no principal's ears have heard, what does not originate in my too human heart.

Once there lived in Israel a man named Joachim, of the tribe of Judah, who herded his own sheep, and feared the boss in simplicity. He had no business beyond his flocks, with which he fed all who feared god, offering a double gift to those who in fear of god labored or taught, and offering a single gift to those who ministered to others. His lambs, his goats, his wool, everything he owned, he divided into three parts. He gave one part to widows, orphans, immigrants, and homeless, a second part to followers of god, and the third part to himself and his household. Because he did so, god multiplied his flocks, until no one from the people of Israel could rival him. He'd begun this practice when he was fifteen. At twenty he married Anna, a daughter of Isachar, from the tribe and family of David, but after twenty years together they still had no children.

Passover was approaching, and the sons of Israel were offering their gifts, but Reuben blocked Joachim's way and said, You are not permitted to offer your gifts first, because you have not fathered any children in Israel. Joachim was very upset, so he went to the book of the twelve tribes of Israel, saying to himself, I will look into the book, to see if I alone have not fathered any children in Israel. Searching, he found that all who were just had brought up children in Israel, but he remembered the patriarch Abraham, how at the end of his life the boss god had given him a son, Isaac. So upset was Joachim that instead of returning to his wife he went out by himself into the desert. He pitched his tent there, and fasted day and night, telling himself, I will not return for food or drink until my boss the god visits me. Prayer will be my food and drink.

His wife Anna lamented with double lamentation and mourned with double mourning, saying, I mourn my widowhood and I mourn my childlessness. Passover was approaching, and her servant girl Judith said to her, How long will you demean your soul? Look, Passover is approaching, so it's not permitted you to grieve. Take this head ribbon that my boss at work gave me: I can't wear it because I'm your servant girl but it's fit for royalty. Anna replied, Go away from me. I didn't do anything, but my boss the god has demeaned me greatly. Maybe some wrongdoer gave this to you, and you've come to make me complicit in your error. But the servant girl Judith said, Why would I curse you just for not listening to me? Your boss the god has closed your womb, keeping you from bearing fruit in Israel. Anna, quite upset, took off her mourning cloak and washed her hair and put on her wedding cloak. In the afternoon she went down to walk in her garden. She saw a laurel tree and sat beneath it, and pausing there she prayed to the master, saying, O god of my fathers, bless me and answer this my entreaty, just as you blessed the womb of Sarah and gave her a son Isaac.

Anna, gazing toward the sky, saw a nest of sparrows in the laurel. She improvised a dirge, singing to herself:

> Aiee, who made me? What womb brought me forth?
> I was born an insult to the sons of Israel.
> They scorned me and mocked me and banished me
> from the temple of my boss the god.
> Aiee, what am I like? I am not like the birds of the sky:
> even the birds of the sky are fertile before you, boss.
> Aiee, what am I like? I am not like the wordless animals:
> even the wordless animals are fertile before you, boss.
> Aiee, what am I like? I am not like the beasts of the earth:
> even the beasts of the earth are fertile before you, boss.
> Aiee, what am I like? I am not like the waters:
> even water, whether still or flowing, blesses you with fish, boss.
> Aiee, what am I like? I am not like this earth,
> for even this earth brings forth fruit in its season and blesses
>   you, boss.

Then, look, an emissary of the boss appeared, speaking to her: Anna, Anna, the boss has answered your entreaty. You will conceive and give birth, and your offspring will be the talk of the whole world. Anna replied, As the boss god lives, whether I give birth to a boy or a girl, I will offer it as a gift to my boss god, and it will serve xer all the days of its life.

And, look, two emissaries arrived, saying to her, Look, Joachim your husband is arriving with his flocks. An emissary of the boss had come down to Joachim and told him, Joachim, Joachim, the boss god has answered your entreaty. Go down from here. Look, your wife Anna will conceive. Immediately Joachim went down and called his shepherds, saying to them, Bring me here ten spotless and unblemished lambs: the ten lambs will be for the boss god. And bring me twelve tender calves, and the twelve calves will be for the priests and elders. And a hundred goats for all the people. Then, look, Joachim arrived with his flocks. And Anna stood at the gate and saw Joachim coming with his flocks and instantly she ran to him and threw her arms around his neck, and said, Now I know the boss god has blessed me greatly, because, look, the widow is no longer a widow, and I the childless one have conceived. On his first day back home, Joachim rested.

The next day Joachim presented his gifts, telling himself, If the boss god is gracious to me, the veneer of the priest will reveal it to me. So Joachim offered his gifts and watched the veneer of the priest as he approached the altar of the boss, and he did not see error in himself. And Joachim said, Now I know that the boss god has been gracious to me and has released me from all my errors. Joachim went down from the temple of the boss justified, and returned to his house. The months were fulfilled for Anna, and in the ninth month when she gave birth, Anna asked the midwife, What have I given birth to? The midwife replied, It's a girl. Anna said, My soul is enlarged today. And she lay down. When the days were completed, Anna bathed herself and gave her breast to the child and named her Mary.

Day by day the child grew stronger. When she was six months old, her mother stood her up on the floor to see if she could stand upright. She walked seven steps to reach the bosom of her mother. Her mother lifted her up, saying to her, As the boss god lives, you will not walk another step on this earth until I take you to the temple of the boss. And she made a sanctuary of her bedroom, and allowed into it nothing common or unclean. She invited the unstained daughters of the Hebrews and they visited her.

When the child had her first birthday, Joachim hosted a great feast and invited the chief priests and the priests and the scribes and the elders and all the people of Israel. Joachim brought the child to the priests, who blessed her, saying, O god of our fathers, bless this child and grant that her name be known forever, to all generations. And all the people replied, So be it, amen. And they brought her to the chief priests, who blessed her, saying, O god of the heights, look down on this child and bless her with an ultimate blessing that has no successor.

Her mother returned the child to the sanctuary of her bedroom and gave her her breast. Improvising a song to the boss god, Anna sang,

> I sing a song to my boss the god,
> because xe has visited me and removed from me the scorn
> of my enemies
> and my boss the god has given me the fruit of xer justice,
> unique to xer, abundant from xer.
> Who will inform the sons of Reuben that Anna is nursing?
> Listen, listen, you twelve tribes of Israel: Anna is nursing.

And she laid the baby down to nap in the sanctuary of her bedroom, and went out to serve others. When the feast had ended, they went away satisfied and they praised the god of Israel.

With the months, the child advanced. When she turned two, Joachim said, Let us go up to the temple of the boss, to fulfill the promise we promised, so that the master not send harm to us or find our gift unacceptable. Anna replied, Let's wait until she's three, so she won't miss her father and mother. Joachim acquiesced: Yes, let's wait.

When the child turned three, Joachim said, Call the unstained daughters of the Hebrews, and let each take a torch and stand it, burning, so that the child not turn back and her heart not retreat from the temple of the boss. They did so and then went up to the temple of the boss. Receiving her, the priest kissed her and blessed her and said, The boss god has magnified your name to all generations. Through you to the end of time the boss god will reveal xer redemption to the sons of Israel.

He set her on the third step of the altar, and the boss god rained grace on her, and she danced on her feet, and the whole house of Israel loved her. Her parents returned amazed, praising and glorifying the master god because the child did not turn back. Mary was in the temple of the boss, tended like a dove, and fed from the hand of an emissary.

Everyone admired Mary, who was only three years old, but walked with so mature a step and spoke so perfectly and praised god so studiously that she seemed not a little girl but an adult. It was as if she were thirty years old, so insistently did she pray, and her face so shone that no one was able to look straight at her. She worked well with wool, and was able to untangle even what older women could not.

She made it a rule for herself to persist in prayer from before dawn until midmorning, to work at her weaving from morning to afternoon, and to return to prayer from afternoon on, until an emissary from the god appeared and gave her food from his hand. In this way she developed more and more in fear of the god. In fact, as the older virgins taught her how to offer praise to the god, she developed such a zeal for goodness that she always managed to be first in the vigils, more expert in the wisdom of the law of the god, more humble in humility, more elegant in singing the psalms of David, more gracious in charity, more pure in purity, more perfect in every virtue. She was constant and unwavering, becoming better and better by the day.

No one ever saw her irritable, no one ever heard her speak ill of anyone. Her every word was so full of grace that in her speech one could recognize the god xerself. Always she persisted in prayer and in study of the law of the god. Of those around her, she was solicitous that none of them should err even in one word, or laugh too loudly, or be hurtful or proud toward one they lived with. Without interruption she blessed the god. So that even another's greeting not distract her from praise of the god, when someone greeted her she returned that greeting with this greeting, God bless. In fact, it was from her that the saints acquired the custom of saying to one another, God bless. Daily she was refreshed only by the food she received from the hand of an emissary, and what the priests of the temple gave her she paid forward to the poor. Often she was seen to speak with emissaries, and they watched over her as a loved one. Any sick person who touched her was immediately restored to health by the touch.

When she turned twelve, the priests met together, saying, Look, Mary has turned twelve in the temple of the boss. What should we do with her, so that she does not pollute the sanctuary of our boss the god? They said to the chief priest, You have stood at the altar of the boss; go in and pray about her, and whatever the boss god reveals to you, we'll do. So the chief priest, carrying the twelve bells, went in to the holy of holies and prayed about her. And look, an emissary of the boss stood before him, saying, Zacharias, Zacharias, go out and assemble from the people the widowers, and have each bring a staff, and the one to whom the boss god gives a sign, she will be his wife. Heralds went out through the whole countryside of Judea and sounded the trumpet of the boss, and all came swiftly.

Joseph set down his adze and went to the assembly. When they had gathered, they approached the priest, carrying their staffs. Receiving the staffs from them, he went into the temple and prayed. Upon finishing the prayer, he picked up the staffs and went out and gave them back. There was no sign on them. Joseph picked up the last staff, and, look, a dove flew out of the staff and alighted on Joseph's head. The priest said to Joseph, You have been chosen to receive into your protection the virgin of the boss. But Joseph protested, saying, I have sons and I'm an old man; she is young. I'll be a laughingstock to the sons of Israel. The priest replied, Joseph, fear your boss the god, and remember all that the god did to Dathan, Abiram, and Korah, how the earth was split open and they were all swallowed up because of their rebellion. Now take care, Joseph, that this does not happen also to your house. Joseph, fearing, received her into his protection, and said to her, Mary, I have received you from the temple of the boss, and now I'm leaving you here in my house. I have to go build some buildings, but I'll return. The boss will protect you.

The priests met together, saying, We'll make a curtain for the temple. So the priest said, Call to me the unstained virgins from the tribe of David. The officers went out and searched and found seven virgins. The priest remembered that the child Mary was from the tribe of David and that she was unstained before the god, so the officers went out and brought her back. They led them into the temple of the boss, and the priest said, Draw lots before me, for who will spin the gold, the pure white, the linen, the silk, the azure, the scarlet, and the true purple. Mary drew the lot for the true purple and the scarlet. Taking them, she returned home. Taking up the scarlet, Mary spun it. She made the purple and the scarlet and brought them to the priest. Receiving them, the priest, blessing her, said, Mary, the boss god has magnified your name, and you will be blessed across all generations of the earth.

Mary took a pitcher and went out to draw water. And look, a voice said to her, Hello, favored one. The boss is with you. You are blessed among women. Mary looked right and left to see where the voice came from. Trembling, she returned to her house and took up the purple and sat in her chair and began to spin the purple. And look, an emissary of the boss stood before her, saying, Don't fear, Mary. You have found favor before the master of all. You will conceive a child by xer word. Hearing this, Mary reflected, asking herself, Am I to conceive a child by the living boss god and give birth like all other women?

But the emissary of the boss said to her, Not so, Mary. The power of god will overshadow you, and therefore the holy one born from you will be called the xon of the highest. And you will call xer by the name Jesus, because xe will preserve xer people from their errors. The boss god will give xer the throne of xer father David, and across the ages xe will rule the house of Jacob, and to xer reign there will be no end. Mary asked the emissary, How will this happen, since I haven't been intimate with a man? In reply the emissary told her, The holy breath will blow over you, and the power of the highest will overshadow you, and therefore the holiness born to you will be called xon of god. And look, your relative Elizabeth also has conceived in her old age, and she who was called infertile is in her sixth month. No word from the god will prove impossible. Mary said, Look, I am the slave of the boss, so let it happen as you say. And the emissary left her.

In the days of Herod's reign over Judea there was a priest named Zachariah, of the priestly order of Abia, and his wife, a descendant of Aaron, whose name was Elizabeth. Both of them were just before the god, blamelessly fulfilling all the commandments and regulations of the boss. But they had no child, because Elizabeth was infertile, and both were well along in years.

As part of his priestly dutiees to the god, it happened that he was assigned to enter the sanctuary of the boss to burn incense. The whole assembly of the people was just outside, praying at the time of incense-burning. An emissary of the boss appeared to him, standing at the right-hand side of the altar of incense. Seeing him, Zachariah was disturbed, and fear overwhelmed him. But the emissary said to him, Don't fear, Zachariah: your prayer has been heard. Your wife Elizabeth will bear you a son, and you will name him John. You will have joy and gladness, and many will celebrate his birth. He will have high standing before the boss. He will drink no wine or liquor, and even while he's in his mother's womb he'll be filled with the holy breath, and he will turn many of the children of Israel toward their boss the god, before whom he himself will go with the breath and strength of Elijah, to turn the hearts of fathers toward their children and the unruly toward the wisdom of the just, preparing a people fit for the boss.

Zachariah said to the emissary, How can I be sure of this? I myself am an old man, and my wife is well along in years. In reply the emissary told him, I am Gabriel, who stands before the god, and I have been sent to speak to you, to deliver this good news. But look, you will be silent, unable to speak until the day this happens, because you didn't believe my words, which in due time will be fulfilled.

Meanwhile, the people were waiting for Zachariah, wondering why he stayed so long in the sanctuary. When he came out, unable to speak to them, they realized that in the sanctuary he had seen a vision. He gestured to them, but could not speak. It happened that when the days of his priestly service were completed he returned home. Not long after that, his wife Elizabeth conceived, and for five months she secluded herself, saying, The boss has done this for me, at last showing me favor by taking away my disgrace in front of others.

Mary arose and traveled to a town in the hill country of Judah, and entered the house of Zachariah and greeted Elizabeth. And it happened that, when Elizabeth heard Mary's greeting, the child in her womb kicked, and Elizabeth was filled with holy breath. Speaking in a loud voice, she said, Blessed are you among women, and blessed is the fruit of your womb. How can this happen to me, that the mother of the boss has come to me? Look, as soon as your voice sounded in my ears, the baby in my womb kicked with gladness. Graceful is she who believes in the fulfillment of what was told her from the boss.

And Mary said,
> My soul extols the boss,
>> and my breath rejoices in the god my preserver,
> because xe has regarded the humble state of xer slave.
>> Look, from now on all generations will call me graceful,
> because the powerful one has done great things for me,
>> and xer name is holy,
> and xer mercy from generation to generation
>> is on those who fear xer.
> Xe has acted with arm strength,
>> scattering those who were arrogant in their minds and hearts.
> Xe has knocked down the powerful from their thrones,
>> and raised up the humble,
> filling the hungry with good things
>> and sending the wealthy away empty-handed.
> Xe has helped xer slave boy Israel,
>> remembering xer mercy,
> as xe promised to our fathers,
>> to Abraham and his offspring forever.

Mary stayed with Elizabeth for three months, and then returned home, and day by day her belly grew. Fearfully, she returned home, and hid herself from the sons of Israel. She was sixteen when these mysteries happened to her.

The time came for Elizabeth's delivery, and she gave birth to a son. Her neighbors and friends heard how the boss had shown great mercy to her, and they rejoiced with her. It happened, on the eighth day when they came to perform the initiation rite, that they called the child Zachariah, giving him his father's name. But in reply his mother said, No, he'll be called John. They said to her, But none of your relatives is called by that name. They gestured to his father, to find out what he wanted the boy to be called. Requesting a tablet, he wrote, His name is John. They all were astonished. Immediately his mouth was opened and his tongue freed, and he spoke, blessing the god. Fear filled all their neighbors, and these things got talked about throughout the hill country of Judea. All who heard these stories stored them in their hearts, asking, because the hand of the boss was on him, What sort of child will this be? His father Zachariah, filled with holy breath, prophesied, saying,

> Blessed be the boss god of Israel
> > because xe has visited xer people and brought them
> > > redemption,
> and has lifted up a horn of preservation for us,
> > in the house of David xer slave boy,
> as xe has declared from the beginning through the mouths
> > of the holy prophets,
> > > to preserve us from our enemies and from the hand of
> > > · all who hate us,
> to enact the mercy promised our fathers,
> > and to remember xer holy covenant,
> the oath xe swore to our father Abraham,
> > to give us, protected from the hands of our enemies,
> fearlessness in serving xer, in piety and justice
> > before xer all the days of our lives.
> And you, child, will be called a prophet of the highest,
> > because you will go before the boss to prepare the way
> > > for xer,
> to offer knowledge of preservation to xer people,
> > in forgiveness of their errors,
> through the tender mercy of our god,
> > by which sunlight from above shines down on us,
> to those who sit in darkness, under the shadow of death,
> > to direct our feet along the path of peace.

And the child grew, acquiring strength of breath, and he stayed in the desert until the day of his presentation to Israel.

Mary was in her sixth month when, look, Joseph returned from his buildings and entered his house and recognized her pregnancy. He struck his face and threw himself to the ground on sackcloth and wept bitterly, saying, How can I face the boss god? What prayer can I say for this girl? I received her from the temple of the boss god as a virgin, but I didn't protect her. Who has deceived me? Who has done this harm in my house and corrupted this virgin? Has the story of Adam repeated itself in me? While Adam was in the hour of praise, the snake came and found Eve alone and deceived her; just so has it happened to me.

Joseph rose up from the sackcloth and called her and said to her, You who are cared for by god, why have you done this? Have you forgotten your boss the god? Why have you demeaned your soul, you who were raised in the holy of holies and fed by the hand of an emissary? But she wept bitterly and insisted, I am clean and have not slept with a man. Joseph replied to her, How then did you get pregnant? She said, As my boss the god lives, I don't know how this happened to me.

Joseph feared greatly and let her alone, debating what to do about her. He said, if I hide her error, I'll be found to be opposing the law of the boss, but if I reveal her to the sons of Israel, I fear that what is in her is from the emissary and I'll be found delivering innocent blood to a death sentence. What should I do with her? I'll send her away from me in secret. Then night overwhelmed him, and, look, an emissary of the boss appeared to him in a dream, saying, Don't fear this child. What is in her is from a breath that is holy. She will bear a xon and you will name xer Jesus, because xe will preserve xer people from their errors. This happened, in order to fulfill what the boss spoke through the prophet, saying,

Look, a virgin will become pregnant and bear a xon,

and they will call xer by the name Emmanuel,

which translates to the god is with us. Rising from sleep, Joseph did as the emissary of the boss had instructed, and took her as his wife, and did not know her until after she had given birth to the xon he called by the name Jesus.

Annas the scribe came to him and asked, Joseph, why have you not appeared before our assembly? He replied, I was tired from my journey and rested the first day back. But Annas turned and recognized Mary's pregnancy. He went running to the priest and said to him, Joseph, the one you spoke for, has egregiously violated the law. The priest asked, How? Annas said, It's the virgin, the one he received from the temple of the boss: he has corrupted her and stolen her marriageability, and not revealed it to the sons of Israel. The priest sought confirmation: Joseph has done this? And Annas the scribe said to him, Send agents, and you'll find the virgin pregnant. The agents went and confirmed what he'd said, and brought her and Joseph to the tribunal.

The chief priest questioned her: Mary, why have you done this? Why have you demeaned your soul and forgotten your boss the god? You who were raised in the holy of holies and fed from the hand of an emissary, you who heard xer hymns and danced before xer, why have you done this? But she wept bitterly, protesting, As my boss god lives, I am clean before xer and have not slept with a man.

The priest said, Joseph, why have you done this? Joseph replied, As the boss my god lives, and by the truth of xer witness, I am clean toward her. The priest pressed him, Don't give false witness; tell the truth. You have stolen her marriageability and not revealed it to the sons of Israel, and not bowed your head to the hand of authority so that your offspring will be blessed.

Joseph stayed silent. The priest said, Give back the virgin you received from the temple of the boss. Joseph began to shed silent tears. The chief priest said, I'll have you both drink the water of testing by the boss, and it will reveal your error to your own eyes. The priest give it to Joseph to drink, and sent him into the desert, but he returned whole. The priest gave it to Mary to drink and sent her into the desert, and she returned whole. And all the people were amazed, because it did not reveal error in either of them. The priest said, If the boss god has not revealed error in you, I don't convict you. He released them, and Joseph and Mary returned home, thanking and praising the god of Israel.

At that time, Caesar Augustus by edict ordered a census, so everyone had to return to their homeland. This census, the first during Cyrinus' rule over Syria, made it necessary for Joseph to travel with Mary to Bethlehem, because Joseph and Mary were of the tribe of Judah and the house and lineage of David. While Joseph and Mary were on the road to Bethlehem, Mary said to Joseph, I see two groups of people in front of me, one weeping and the other celebrating. In response to her, Joseph said, Sit and hold onto the donkey and say no more nonsense to me. Then a beautiful child dressed in bright clothes appeared in front of them and said to Joseph, Why are you calling nonsense the words you heard about the two groups of people? She sees the Jewish people weeping because they are withdrawing from god, and the other people celebrating because they are advancing toward the boss, as promised to your fathers Abraham, Isaac, and Jacob. The time has arrived when from the seed of Abraham the good news will go out to all people.

The child, having said this, ordered the donkey to stop, and told Mary to get down from the animal and enter a cave that was always dark, never having seen the light of day. But when Mary entered, the whole cave shone with great splendor, as if the sun had entered it, so that the whole cave gave a bright light, and it was like midday, so brightly did the divine light illuminate the whole cave. The light did not dim day or night, until Mary gave birth to a xon, whom the emissaries surrounded at birth. As soon as xe was born, xe stood on xer feet and they worshiped xer, saying, Glory to the highest god, and to earth the peace of people of good will.

Joseph, discovering Mary with the infant she had given birth to, said to her, I have brought you Zahel, a midwife. Look, she's standing at the mouth of the cave, but because of the splendor she's not able to enter. Hearing this, Mary smiled. But Joseph instructed her, Don't smile, but prepare for her to examine you to see if you need medicine from her. Mary invited her to enter. When Mary allowed the examination, the midwife cried out in a loud voice, Big boss, have mercy! Before now, nothing like this has been heard of or thought possible. Her breasts are full of milk and the child demonstrates the virginity of xer mother. No stain of blood is present on the newborn, and the mother appears to have felt no pain. A virgin has given birth, and after the birth has continued to be a virgin.

Hearing Zahel's exclamation, a midwife named Salome said, I sure won't believe that unless I see for myself. Approaching Mary, Salome said to her, Allow me to examine you so I can determine whether it's true what Zahel tells me. Mary permitted herself to be examined, but as soon as Salome withdrew her right hand from the examination, the hand withered and she began to suffer intensely from the pain, and to cry out, weeping and saying, Boss, you know I've always feared you and cared for all the poor without asking to be repaid. I've demanded nothing of the widow and orphan, and no beggar has gone away from me empty-handed. But look, I'm suffering now for my disbelief, because I tested your virgin, who gave birth to light and after the birth remained a virgin.

Even as she spoke, a resplendent young man appeared at her side, saying, Go to the infant and adore xer and touch xer with your right hand. Xe'll heal you, because xe is the preserver of all who put their hope in xer. Immediately Salome went and, adoring the infant, she touched the hem of the blanket in which xe was wrapped, and immediately her hand was healed. She went outside then and began to cry out, to declare the great power she'd seen and what she'd suffered and how she'd been healed, so that by her declaration many came to believe.

In that same region there were some shepherds staying out in the fields to guard their flocks at night. An emissary of the boss confronted them and the glory of the boss shimmered around them, and they feared with deep fear. But the emissary said to them, Don't be afraid. Look, I'm bringing you good news that will bring great joy to all the people, that this day there is born for you in the city of David a preserver, who is the salve, the boss. And this is your sign: you will find the child wrapped in rags and lying in a hay crib. Suddenly there was with the emissary a whole regiment from the sky praising the god and saying,

Glory to the highest god,
and to earth the peace of people of good will.

It happened, after the emissaries had returned to the sky, that the shepherds conferred with one another: Let's go to Bethlehem and see for ourselves this thing that has happened, that the boss has alerted us to. So they went quickly, and found Mary and Joseph, and the child lying in a hay crib. Seeing it, they spread around what had been told them about the child, and everyone who heard it was amazed by what the shepherds told them. But Mary treasured all these tellings, collecting them in her heart. The shepherds returned, glorifying and worshiping the god for their having heard and seen all the things that had been told them.

On the third day after the birth of the boss, Mary left the cave and entered a stable and placed the baby in a feed trough, and an ox and an ass bent to their knees, adoring xer. Then was fulfilled the statement declared by the prophet Isaiah, *The ox recognizes its owner and the ass the food trough of its boss.* These animals stayed near xer, incessantly adoring xer. Then was fulfilled the statement declared by the prophet Habbakuk, *Between two animals you will make yourself known.* Joseph and Mary with the infant stayed in that same place for three days.

When the eight days before the initiation rite had been fulfilled, they gave xer the name Jesus, the name assigned by the emissary even before xe'd been conceived in the womb. And when the days were fulfilled for xer purification according to the law of Moses, they took xer to Jerusalem to present xer to the boss, and to give the sacrifice stipulated by the law of the boss, a pair of turtledoves or two young pigeons.

There was also in the temple a man of god, a prophet and a just man, named Simeon, who was 112 years old. He had received from god a promise that he would not taste death until he had seen the salve the xon of god in the flesh. When he saw the infant, exclaiming in a loud voice he said, God has visited xer people, god has kept xer promise. Intently he adored the infant. Then he picked xer up in xer blanket and adored xer and kissed xer feet and said, Now, boss, send away your servant in peace, because my eyes have seen your salvation, which you prepared in sight of all people, light for a revelation to all peoples and glory for your people, Israel.

There was also in the temple of the boss Anna, daughter of Phanuel, who had lived with her husband for seven years after her virginity. She was a widow now, eighty-four years old, who, never leaving the temple of the boss, devoted herself to fasts and prayers. She too approached to adore the infant, saying that in xer is the redemption of the age: The xon is in every way perfect: xe is the word the voice spoke; xe arrives from the heights; xe contains within xerself the name; xe is light. Xe reveals timeless things and makes the unknown known. Xe reveals hermetic, secret things, addressing those who inhabit the silence of the first thought. Xe reveals xerself to those under darkness, and shows xerself to those within the abyss. To those who secure the hidden stores xe tells inexplicable mysteries, and xe tells unrestatable truths to those who become xons of light.

⊥⊦
⊤⊦

In the second year, sages from the east, bringing precious gifts, came to Jerusalem to worship, in urgent inquiry asking the Jews, Where is the king who has been born to us? Even in the east, we saw xer star, and have journeyed here to worship xer. This news reached King Herod. It terrified him, so he summoned the scribes and Pharisees and the teachers of the people, and he asked where the prophets had predicted the birth of the salve would occur. They told him, In Bethlehem of Judea, because it is written this way by the prophet:

And you, Bethlehem, in the land of Judah,

are not least among the principalities of Judah,

because from you will come a ruler

who will shepherd my people Israel.

Then King Herod called to him the sages and thoroughly interrogated them about how the star had appeared to them, and he sent them to Bethlehem, saying, Go, and once you have worshiped xer, report back to me so that I too can go to worship xer.

As the sages went their way the star appeared, and as if guiding them it stayed in front of them until they arrived at where xe was. When they saw the star stop, the sages joyed with great joy, and entering they saw the child Jesus sitting on Mary's lap. Opening their trunk, they gave rich gifts to Mary and Joseph, and to the child xerself they offered a single nugget of singular gold. One offered this gold, another frankincense, the third myrrh. When they thought to return to King Herod, they were warned in a dream of what Herod intended. Then they worshiped the infant again and with great joy returned home along a different route.

When King Herod realized he'd been duped by the sages, his heart got hot and he sent out soldiers to all the roads, wanting to capture them. Unable to find any trace of them, he sent soldiers to Bethlehem to kill every infant two years old and younger, to include the time of birth told him by the sages. But one day before Herod issued this order, look, an emissary of the boss appeared to Joseph in a dream, saying, Get up and take the child and xer mother and flee to Egypt and stay there until I tell you, because Herod will search for the child, to kill xer. So he got up and at night took the child and xer mother and took off for Egypt, and stayed there until the death of Herod, in this way fulfilling what had been spoken about the boss by the prophet, saying, *Out of Egypt I have called my xon.*

When they reached a cave where they could pause and cool themselves, Mary got down from the donkey and sat, holding Jesus in her lap. Going with them along the road were three slave boys, and one slave girl for Mary. And look, suddenly many dragons emerged from the cave. The slaves, seeing them, screamed. Then the boss, never mind xe hadn't even turned two, awoke and got to xer feet and stood facing the dragons, who worshiped xer and then retreated. This fulfilled what was said by the prophet who wrote the psalm that says, *Dragons and all from the abyss praise the boss of the earth.*

Jesus the boss the salve, though only an infant, walked alongside them so as not to be a burden. Mary and Joseph said to one another, Better that those dragons kill us than that they harm the child. Jesus instructed them, Don't consider me a child; I was born already fully adult, and it was given me to tame all kinds of wild beasts.

Similarly, lions and leopards worshiped xer, escorting xer through the desert wherever xe went with Mary and Joseph, going before them showing the way, and being deferential, bowing their heads with great reverence and demonstrating their servitude by waving their tails. The first day that Mary saw lions, leopards, and various wild monsters surrounding them, she was very fearful. The infant Jesus, facing her, smiled, and with a calming voice said, Don't fear, mother, they follow closely not to harm you but to serve you. Xer words removed the fear from her heart.

So lions walked alongside donkeys and oxen, the beasts of burden carrying the humans' necessaries, and whenever they made camp, the animals would graze. Tame goats, too, showed up and followed them through Judea, walking fearlessly right alongside wolves. One was not afraid of the next, and none was harmed by another in any way. This fulfilled what Isaiah wrote: *Wolves will pasture with sheep, and lion and ox eat hay side by side.* They had two oxen with them as pack animals on their journey, and lions directed them on the way of our boss Jesus the salve, whose necessaries they carried.

It happened after this, on the third day of their progress, that Mary wearied from so much desert sun, and seeing a palm tree she wanted to rest a little while in its shade. Joseph swiftly led her to the palm and helped her down from the donkey. When Mary had sat down, she looked up to the crown of the palm and saw how full of fruit it was, and exclaimed, Oh to be able to reach up and pluck some fruit from this palm! Joseph said to her, I can't believe you're saying this when you can see how tall the palm is. While you're thinking about the fruit of the palm, I'm thinking about the water that our water skins no longer hold, because we have nowhere to refill them so that we can quench our thirst.

Then the infant Jesus, sitting on xer virgin mother's lap, yelled at the palm tree, commanding it, Bend down, tree, and refresh my mother with your fruit. As soon as xe spoke, the palm inclined its crown to Mary, and they all gathered fruit from it and were refreshed. After all its fruit had been gathered, the tree remained inclined, waiting for a command to rise from the one who had commanded it to incline. Then Jesus said to it, Rise, palm, and be sturdy, and stand among the trees in the paradise of my fother, and open from your roots hidden springs, so that we can drink from the flowing water. Immediately the palm stood erect, and from its roots water flowed, clear and cold and sweet. Seeing the flowing springs of water, they all joyed with great joy, and beasts and humans together drank, giving thanks to the god.

The next day they set out. At the hour of departure, Jesus, turning to the palm, said, I give you this privilege, palm, that one of your branches will be transported by my emissaries and planted in the paradise of my fother, and I confer on you this benediction, that all contest victors will be told, You have won the palm. As xe was speaking, look, an emissary of the boss appeared, stationed above the palm. After plucking one of the branches, it flew away. When they saw this, they all fell face down to the ground as if they were dead. Then Jesus, consoling them, said, Why has fear taken hold of your hearts? Do you not understand that this palm I've had transported will be readied for all the saints in the place of delight, just as it was readied for you in this desert?

Joseph said to xer, Boss, to keep this heat from prostrating us, if you want we can follow the seaside road, passing through coastal towns where we can rest. Jesus replied, Don't fear, Joseph, I'll shorten the distance from camp so that, even though normally it would take thirty strenuous days, now you will reach your destination in a single day. Even as xe was speaking, look, they saw before them the mountains of Egypt and its plains.

Joying and exulting, they entered one of the cities, called Sohennen. Knowing no one there who would take them in, they entered what in this Egyptian city was considered the primary temple. In this temple stood 365 idols, to each of which these sacrilegious people gave honor on its own day.

It happened that when Mary with the infant entered the temple, this imaginary universe collapsed, and all the idols, thrown face down, revealed themselves to be nothing. This fulfilled what the prophet said: *Look, the boss will arrive light as a cloud, and all the handiwork of the Egyptians will move out of xer way.*

When Aphrodisius got this news, he went to the temple with his whole army and with all his friends and familiars. All the priests of the temple hoped he would say nothing against the cause of the collapse. When he entered the temple and saw that what he'd heard was true, immediately he approached Mary and adored as boss the infant Mary held in her lap. After adoring xer, he addressed his whole army and all his friends, and said, If this one were not the boss of these our gods, they would not have fallen down before xer, and they would not prostrate themselves in xer breath and proclaim xer their boss. If we ourselves, therefore, seeing what our gods have done, are not careful to do the same, we all risk incurring xer indignation and being destroyed, as happened to Pharaoh the king of Egypt who ruled in the days when the god performed great miracles in Egypt and liberated xer people by xer powerful hand.

After Herod's death, look, an emissary of the boss appeared in a dream to Joseph in Egypt, saying, Get up and take the child and xer mother and go to the land of Israel, because the ones who sought the child's soul have died. So he got up and took the child and xer mother and entered into the land of Israel. But when he heard that Archelaus ruled in Judea in place of his father Herod,

Joseph was afraid to go there. Warned by a dream, he set off for the region of Galilee, and arriving there he set up house in a city called Nazareth, in this way fulfilling what had been spoken by the prophets, that xe would be called a Nazarene. The child grew and became strong, filled with wisdom, and the favor of god was upon xer.

When the child Jesus was five years old, playing at the ford of a stream, having diverted some flowing water into pools xe made it instantly clean, commanding this with a single word. Xe made some mud, and from it molded twelve sparrows. Xe did all this on the sabbath. Many other children were with xer, playing. When a certain adult saw that while playing Jesus made something on the sabbath, he went right away and told on xer to xer father, Joseph: Hey, your child is at the stream, and xe's taken mud and molded twelve sparrows, profaning the sabbath. When Joseph went to the place to see, he scolded Jesus, exclaiming, Why are you doing on the sabbath what you're not supposed to do? Jesus clapped xer hands and cried out to the sparrows, Go! The sparrows took off and flew away, chirping. The Jews who saw this were astounded, and went off to tell their leaders what they'd seen Jesus do.

The son of Annas the scribe was standing there with Joseph. Taking a willow branch, he scattered the water Jesus had gathered. Seeing this, Jesus got mad and said to him, You're unfair, insolent, and ignorant. What did the pools of water do to you? Well, now you'll wither like a tree, and never bear leaves or roots or fruit. Immediately the child withered completely, and Jesus went back to Joseph's house. The parents of the withered boy picked him up, mourning his lost youth, and brought the body to Joseph, reprimanding him: What kind of child do you have, who does things like this?

Later on xe was walking through town and a boy running by bumped against xer shoulder. Irritated, Jesus said to him, You won't run on this street anymore. Immediately the child dropped dead. Some who saw it happen exclaimed, Where did this child come from, whose every saying is a deed done? Confronting Joseph, the parents of the dead child blamed him, saying, You can't have such a child and live with us in this town unless you teach xer to bless rather than to curse. Xe's killing our children!

Calling Jesus aside, Joseph scolded xer, saying, Why are you doing these things? These people are suffering; they hate us and ostracize us. Jesus replied, Knowing these words aren't yours, I won't respond to them, for your sake. But these others will get what they deserve. Immediately those who had accused xer were blinded. Those who saw this, afraid and upset, said of xer, Everything xe says, good or bad, miraculously happens. Seeing what Jesus had done, Joseph jumped up and grabbed xer ear and tweaked it hard. The child was furious, and said to him, It wasn't enough for you to seek and not to find; you had to do something stupid. Don't you get it that I'm yours? Don't piss me off.

A teacher named Zacchaeus, standing not far off, overheard Jesus saying these things to xer father, and was amazed that a mere child would say such things. A few days later he approached Joseph and said to him, You have a bright kid; xe has smarts. Give xer to me so xe'll learn xer letters, and while I'm teaching xer letters I'll teach xer everything xe should know, including how to respect xer elders and defer to them as xer ancestors and parents, and how to get along with kids xer own age. He pronouced for xer all the letters, alpha through omega, with exaggerated clarity. But looking straight at the teacher Zacchaeus, Jesus said to him, You who don't know alpha in its essence, how can you teach others beta? Hypocrite, first teach something worth knowing about alpha, and then we'll believe what you say about beta. And xe began to pose the teacher questions about the first letter, questions the teacher couldn't answer. While others listened, the child challenged Zacchaeus, Listen, teacher, to the structure of the first letter. Note that it has lines, a middle stroke that joins two outer strokes that themselves rise and converge and return, three proportional lines that depend on and support one another. Those are the lines of the alpha.

When the teacher Zacchaeus heard the child expounding such interpretations, so many and so allegorical, of the first letter, he was speechless at such insight and exposition, and said to those present, Aiee, I'm speechless and sunk, I've shamed myself by taking on this child. I beg you, brother Joseph, take xer away. I can't bear the severity of xer gaze, or pin down one word. This is no earthly child, xe can even tame fire. Xe was born before the world was created. To xer the fother entrusted all things, what was, what is, and what will be. What belly bore xer, what womb sustained xer, I don't know. Aiee, friend, xe outthinks me, I can't keep pace with xer understanding. I've been fooling myself; I'm a loser three times over. I sought a student but found a teacher. I'm filled with shame, friends, because even though I'm old I've been outdone by a child. I'll fall ill and die over this child; already I can't look xer in the eye. When everyone says I've been shown up by a small child, what can I say back? How can I explain what xe said about the measure of the first letter? I don't know, friends. I can't tell up from down. So I ask you, brother Joseph, to take xer back home. Whatever great thing xe is, a god or an emissary, I don't know what to say.

While the Jews were consoling Zacchaeus, Jesus laughed out loud and said, Now let what is yours bear fruit, and let the blind in heart see. I have come from above to provoke them and to call them to what is above, as instructed by the one who for your sake sent me. As soon as the child stopped speaking, all who had been cursed by xer were healed, but from then on no one dared anger xer, in case xe curse and cripple them.

Another time, when Jesus was playing on the roof of a house, one of the children playing with xer fell from that rooftop and died. Seeing this, the other children scattered, and only Jesus remained. When the parents of the one who had died arrived, they accused Jesus and threatened xer. Jesus jumped down off the rooftop and stood beside the corpse of the child, and shouting in a loud voice said, Zeno (that was the child's name), rise up and tell me, did I throw you down? And he stood right up and said, No, boss, you didn't throw me down, but you did raise me up. Struck by seeing this, the parents of the child praised the god for making this sign happen, and they worshiped Jesus.

A few days later a young man, splitting wood in a corner, caught a glancing blow with the ax, splitting open his foot. Bleeding badly, he was about to die. The commotion drew a crowd, and Jesus too ran to the spot. Pushing through the crowd, xe took hold of the young man's hurt foot, and instantly it was healed. Xe said to the

the young man, Stand up now, split the wood, and remember me. Seeing this happen, the crowd worshiped the child, saying, Truly the breath of god inhabits this child.

When Jesus was six, xer mother handed xer a pitcher and sent xer to draw some water and bring it back home. But, knocked around in the crowd, the water pitcher broke. So Jesus loosened the cloak xe was wearing, and filled it and brought it to xer mother. Seeing this sign that had happened, xer mother kissed xer, and she kept to herself the mysteries she saw xer perform.

Joseph sent James to gather some wood and bring it home, and the child Jesus followed along. While James was collecting the wood, a snake bit his hand. While he was stretched out on the ground dying, Jesus approached and blew on the snakebite. Instantly the pain stopped, the creature burst, and James was restored to health.

Later on, an infant in Joseph's neighborhood got sick and died, and his mother wept bitterly. Hearing this loud grief and commotion, Jesus ran there quickly. Finding the child dead, xe touched its breast and said, I charge you, little baby, not to die but to live and be with your mother. Immediately the infant opened its eyes and laughed. Jesus said to the woman, Take him and give him milk and remember me. Seeing this, the crowd standing there was amazed, and said, Truly this child is a god or an emissary of god, because xer every word is an accomplished fact. And Jesus went off to play with the other children.

Walking once with xer mother across the city square, Jesus saw a teacher teaching some children. Twelve sparrows flurried down from the wall, bickering, and tumbled into the teacher's lap. Seeing this, Jesus laughed. The teacher, noticing xer laugh, was filled with anger, and said, What's so funny? Jesus replied, Listen, a widow is on her way here carrying what little wheat she can afford, but when she gets here she'll stumble and spill the wheat. These sparrows are fighting over how many grains each will get. Jesus didn't leave until what he'd predicted had occurred. The teacher, seeing that Jesus' words became accomplished deeds, wanted to have xer run out of town, along with xer mother.

One time, in planting season, the child went out with xer father to sow wheat in their field. While xer father sowed, little Jesus planted a single seed. But when it was reaped and threshed, it yielded a hundred bushels, and xe called all the poor people from their village to the threshing floor and gave them the wheat, and Joseph took what was left over. Jesus was eight when xe performed this sign.

Xer father was a carpenter, and back then he made plows and yokes. He got an order from a rich man to make a bed for him. When one of the slats, a cross-piece, came up short, he didn't know what to do, but the child Jesus said to xer father Joseph, Line this board up next to one that's the right length. Joseph did as the child said. Jesus stood at one end, and taking hold of the shorter board stretched it to match the longer. Seeing this, xer father Joseph was amazed, and embracing the child he kissed xer and said, I am blessed that the god gave me this child.

Every year xer parents went to Jerusalem for the celebration of Passover. When xe was twelve they went, as was customary. They fulfilled the days, but when they started their return trip, Jesus stayed behind in Jerusalem, without xer parents' knowing it. After a whole day on the road, when they'd assumed xe was in the caravan, they looked for xer among their relatives and friends, but when they didn't find xer, they returned to Jerusalem, looking for xer. Only after three days did they find xer, in the temple, sitting among the teachers, listening to them and their questioning. Everyone who heard xer was amazed at xer understanding and xer replies to them. Xer parents were shocked when they saw xer, and xer mother said to xer, Xon, why have you done this to us? Your father and I were frantic with worry, looking for you. Xe said to them, Why were you having to search? You didn't know I'd be in my fother's place? But they didn't understand the riddle xe was posing them. Xe returned with them to Nazareth, and was obedient to them, and xer mother secured all xer sayings in her heart. Jesus increased in wisdom and in height and in divine and human favor.

There was a man, sent from god, whose name was John. He came as a witness, to bear witness to the light, so that through him everyone would believe. He was not himself the light, but bore witness of the light. The true light that illuminates every person was coming into the world. Xe was in the world, and the world was made through xer, but the world didn't know xer. Xe came to xer own, but xer own did not receive xer. To those who did receive xer, those who believed in xer name, xe gave entitlement to become children of god, born not of blood or of willful flesh or of a willful person, but of god.

And the word became flesh and pitched tent among us, and we have seen its glory, the glory of the onlyborn of the fother, full of grace and truth. John bore witness to xer, and cried out, saying, This is xe of whom I said, The one who comes after me exceeds me, because xe existed before me. From xer fullness we all receive grace upon grace. The law was given by Moses, but grace and truth came to be through Jesus the salve. No one has seen god, ever: the onlyborn god who is in the bosom of the fother describes her. Xe is the one who may rightfully be called *preserver*, the *redeemer*, the *satisfaction*, the *beloved*, *advocate*, *salve*, and *light of the lit*, in accordance with xer origins and xer fulfillment of the roles xe has assumed. But what name better suits xer than the *xon*, the name we familiarly use, since xe is the knowledge of the fother of the known? Xer fother is the one, the only true fother, invisible, unknowable, incomprehensible in xer essence, wholly divine in will and in grace, allowing xerself in the xon to be seen, known, and comprehended. Our preserver became, in voluntary compassion, what those for whose sake xe appeared had become in involuntary passion, flesh and soul. Xe let xerself be born as a child with body and soul. All the other conditions that the fallen share, xe too assumed, except that xe was conceived without error, stain, and corruption. Xe came into being from the luminous vision and enduring thought of the word.

When the Jews sent priests and Levites from Jerusalem to ask him, Who are you?, John professed, I am not the salve. And they asked him, What then? Are you Elijah? But he said, I'm not. Are you the prophet? But he answered, No. They said to him, Who are you? So we can answer those who sent us, what do you assert about yourself? He said, as the prophet Isaiah had said,

I am one voice bawling in the desert,
Clear a path for the boss.

The ones who'd been sent were from the Pharisees, and they asked him, Why do you baptize, if you're not the salve or Elijah or the prophet? John answered them, saying, I baptize in water. There stands among you one you don't recognize, the one who comes after me, whose sandal strap I'm not worthy to loosen. These things took place in Bethany, beyond the Jordan, where John was baptizing.

The next day he saw Jesus coming toward him and said, Look, the lamb of the god, who takes on xerself the error of the world. This is the one of whom I said, one comes after me who exceeds me because xe existed before me. This is the one called the xon, the one that those who recognize that xe exists see that they seek, the one in whom resides the fother they cannot describe or conceive, the one born first. No one can conceive of xer or think xer through, or approach the pace of xer exalted pre-existence. But all the names applied to xer deferentially are traces matched to the capacity of the worshiper. Xe is all unfalsified names, the one I call the form of the formless, the body of the bodiless, the face of the invisible, the word of the inexpressible, the thought of the inconceivable, the inexaustible spring, the roots of the rooted, the god of the attentive, the light of the lit, the love of the loved, the providence of those provided for, the wisdom of the wise, the power of the empowered, the gathering of the gathered, the revelation of the revealed, the eyes of those who see, the breath of those who breathe, the life of those who live, the unity of the united. I didn't know xer, but so that xe be revealed to Israel, that's why I came baptizing in water. And John bore witness, saying, I saw the breath coming down as a dove from the sky and lighting on xer. I didn't know xer, but the one who sent me to baptize in water told me, The one on whom you see the breath coming down as a dove and remaining on xer, that is the one who baptizes in holy breath. And I saw and I bear witness that this is the xon of the god.

It happened in those days that Jesus came from Nazareth of Galilee and was baptized by John in the Jordan. As soon as xe came up out of the water xe saw the skies split open and the breath descended onto her like a dove. A voice came from the sky, You are my beloved xon; I am proud of you.

Immediately the breath drove Jesus into the desert, to be tested by the devil. Xe fasted for forty days and forty nights, and afterward was hungry. Approaching, the tester said to xer, If you are xon of the god, tell these stones to become bread. In reply xe said, It is written,

> A human does not live by bread only,
>> but by every saying that comes out of the mouth of god.

Then the devil took xer to the holy city and stood xer on the pinnacle of the temple, and said to xer, If you are xon of the god, throw yourself down. After all, it is written,

> Xe will command xer emissaries concerning you,
>> and they'll hold you in their hands,
> so that you don't even stub your toe on a stone.

Jesus said to him, Again it is written, *You are not to test your boss the god.* Again the devil took xer up to a very high mountain and showed xer all the kingdoms of the world in their glory, and said to xer, I give you all of these, if you will kneel to me in worship. But Jesus said to him, Go away, Satan. It is written,

> Worship your boss the god,
>> and serve only xer.

Then the devil left xer, and look, emissaries came and tended xer.

╬

Returning from the desert, as Jesus passed along the Sea of Galilee, xe saw Simon and Simon's brother Andrew casting a net into the sea. They were fishers. Jesus said to them, Follow me and I will make you fishers for humans. Immediately they left their nets and followed xer. Going along a little farther, xe saw James the son of Zebedee and his brother John, in a boat mending their nets. Xe called them. They left their father Zebedee in the boat with the hired hands, and followed xer.

On the third day there was a wedding in Cana of Galilee, and Jesus' mother was there. Jesus and xer apprentices had been invited also. When the wine was gone, Jesus' mother said to xer, They're out of wine. Jesus said to her, Woman, what's that to you or me? My hour has not come yet. Xer mother told the servers, Do whatever xe tells you. There were six stone water jars there for ritual washing, each holding many liters. Jesus said to the servers, Fill the water jars with water. So they filled them to the brim. Xe told them, Draw some out now, and take it to the headwaiter. They did. When the headwaiter had tasted the water that had been turned into wine, he didn't know where it had come from, though the servers who had drawn the water knew. The headwaiter called the groom over and said to him, Everyone serves the fine wine first, and after people are affected by their drinking turn to the worse wine, but you have kept the good wine until now. Right there in Cana of Galilee, Jesus performed this first of xer signs, and revealed xer glory, and xer apprentices believed in xer.

After this xe went down to Capernaum, xe and xer mother and brothers and xer apprentices, and stayed a few days. While xe was in Jerusalem for the festival of Passover, many believed in xer name, seeing the signs xe performed, but Jesus did not believe in them because xe knew them all, and needed no one to inform xer about humanity, because xe knew what is in a human.

One of the Pharisees, named Nicodemus, a principal of the Jews, came to xer at night and said to xer, Rabbi, we know that you have come from god as a teacher; no one could perform the signs you perform if the god were not with xer. In reply, Jesus said to him, Truly I tell you, one who wasn't born at the beginning is not able to see the realm of the god. Nicodemus said to xer, How can a man be born when he's old? Can he enter his mother's womb a second time and be born? Jesus answered, Truly I tell you, one who wasn't born of water and wind is not able to enter into the realm of the god. What is born of the flesh is flesh; what is born of the breath is breath. Don't be surprised that I tell you you must be born at the beginning. The breath breathes the way it wants to, and you hear the sound of it, but don't know where it comes from or where it goes. That's how it is with all who are born of the breath. In reply, Nicodemus asked xer, How can this be? That flesh derives from breath is a marvel, but that breath derives from body is a marvel of marvels. I marvel at how such wealth can inhabit such poverty. In answer, Jesus said to him, Are you a teacher of Israel but don't know these things? Truly, truly I tell you, we speak of what we know and testify to what we've seen, but you don't receive our testimony. If you don't believe what I tell you about the things of the earth, how will you believe what I told you about things of the sky? And no one has gone up to the sky except the one who came down from the sky, the xon of humanity. Just as Moses lifted up a snake in the desert, so must the xon of humanity be lifted up, so that all who believe on xer will have timeless life.

So much did the god love the world, that xe gave xer only xon so that all who believe in xer will not fall into ruin but have timeless life. The god did not send the xon into the world to judge the world but so that through xer the world would be preserved. One who believes in xer will not be judged, but one who does not believe has been judged already, because that one has not believed in the name of the only xon of the god. This is the judgment, that the light has come into the world and humans loved the darkness rather than the light, because their works were worthless. All who do base things hate the light, and don't move toward the light, so that their works will not be exposed. But those who perform the truth move toward the light, to show that their works were done under the god.

After this, Jesus and xer apprentices went into the land of Judea, where xe lingered among the people, and baptized. John, too, was baptizing, at Aenon near Salim, because there was plenty of water there, and people were coming to be baptized. John had not yet been tossed into prison. When a disagreement arose between some of John's apprentices and one of the Judeans, they came to John and said to him, Rabbi, the one who was with you across the Jordan, to whom you attested, that same one baptizes, and everyone's coming to xer. In reply, John said to them, a person can't receive anything not given to him from the sky. You yourselves are my witnesses that I said, I am not the salve, but the one sent before xer. The one who takes the bride is the groom, but the best man, who stands next to him and hears his vow, rejoices at the groom's voice. That joy is mine, now fulfilled. Xe must wax; I must wane.

The one who comes from above is above all. The one who is from the earth is of the earth and speaks of the earth. The one who comes from the sky speaks of the sky: xe testifies to what xe has seen and heard, but no one receives xer testimony. The one who *does* receive xer testimony certifies that the god is true. The gospel of truth is joy for those who, given grace, know the fother of truth through the power of the word that flows from the fullness of the fother's thought and mind. *Preserver* names the work the word does, redeeming those who had not known the fother. *Gospel* names the revelation of hope through which seekers find the sought. The one sent from god lilts the words of the god, because xe does not give the breath partially. The fother loves the xon, and has given everything into xer hand. The one who believes in the xon has timeless life, but the one who disobeys the xon will not see life: the anger of the god awaits him.

When Jesus learned that the Pharisees had heard that Jesus makes and baptizes more apprentices than John (though Jesus xerself did not baptize; xer apprentices did), xe left Judea and went again into Galilee. Xe had to pass through Samaria, so xe came to a town named Sychar, near the plot of land that Jacob gave his son Joseph. Jacob's well was there, so Jesus, exausted by xer journey, sat down at the well. It was around noon.

A woman from Samaria came to draw water. Jesus said to her, Give me a drink. Xer apprentices had gone into town to buy food. The Samaritan woman asked xer, How dare you, a Jew, ask for a drink from me, a Samaritan woman? (Jews don't associate with Samaritans.) In reply, Jesus said to her, If you knew the gift of the god, and who it is who says to you, Give me a drink, you'd have asked xer and xe'd have given you living water. She said to xer, Boss, you have nothing to draw with and the well is deep; where will you get this living water? Are you greater than our father Jacob, who drank from this well himself, along with his children and his flocks? In reply, Jesus told her, All who drink this water get thirsty again, but the one who drinks the water I give her won't get thirsty again, ever. The water I give will become in her a spring of water flowing into timeless life. The woman said to xer, Boss, give me this water, so I won't be thirsty or have to keep coming here to draw.

Xe told her, Go, call your husband and come back here. In answer, the woman said to xer, I don't have a husband. Jesus said to her, That's a pretty way to say it, I don't have a husband, since you've had five husbands, and the one you have now isn't your husband. You're not kidding. The woman said to xer, Boss, I can tell you're a prophet. Our fathers worshiped on this hill, but you say Jerusalem is the place to worship. Jesus said to her, Believe me, woman, the hour is coming when you will worship the fother neither on this hill nor in Jerusalem. You worship what you don't know; we worship what we do know, the preservation that is from the Jews. But the hour is coming, and is now, when the true worshipers will worship the fother in breath and truth, for the fother seeks such people to worship xer. The god is breath, and those who would worship xer must worship in breath and truth. Truth, in existence from the beginning, is sown everywhere. Many see it being sown; few see it being reaped. The woman said to xer, I know that the messiah is coming who is called the salve; when xe comes, xe will report everything to us. Jesus told her, I, the one speaking to you, am xer.

Just then the apprentices returned to xer, and were amazed that xe was speaking with a woman, but no one asked, What do you want and why are you speaking with her? The woman left her water jar and went back into town and told the people, Come, see a person who has told me everything I've ever done; is xe not the salve? They left town and came out to see xer.

Meanwhile, the apprentices urged xer, saying, Rabbi, eat. But xe said to them, I have food to eat that you don't know about. The apprentices asked one another, No one brought xer something to eat? Jesus said to them, My food is to do the will of the one who sent me, and to complete xer work. Don't you say, Four months more, and then comes harvest? Look, I say to you, raise your eyes and look at the fields, how ripe they are for harvest. Already the reaper is earning wages and gathering grain for timeless life, so that sower and reaper may celebrate together. About this the saying holds true, One sows and another reaps. I've sent you to reap what you haven't worked for. Others have labored, and you're benefiting from their troubles.

Many Samaritans from that town believed in xer because of the account of the woman who testified, Xe told me everything I've ever done. So when the Samaritans came to xer, they invited xer to stay with them, and xe stayed two days. And many believed because of xer word, and said to the woman, Now we believe not because of what you told us but because we have heard and seen for ourselves that xe is truly the preserver of the world.

After those two days, xe left there for Galilee. (Jesus xerself had testified that a prophet is given no respect in the prophet's own homeland.) When xe arrived in Galilee, the Galileans welcomed xer, having seen all xe had done in Jerusalem at the festival, because they themselves had been at the festival.

☦

Herod had John arrested and imprisoned, to satisfy Herodias, his brother Philip's wife, whom he had married. John had warned Herod, It's not right for you to have your brother's wife. So Herodias resented him, and wanted to kill him but could not. Herod feared John, recognizing him as a just and holy man, and kept him in custody.

When John, in prison, heard of the works of the salve, he sent two of his apprentices to ask, Are you the anticipated one, or should we look toward someone else? In reply, Jesus said to them, Whoever is near me is near the fire, but whoever is far from me is outside the realm. Go and report to John what you hear and see: the blind see, the lame walk, the leprous are healed, the deaf hear, the dead are raised up, and the poor get good news. Blessed is the one who does not stumble over me.

As they were going away, Jesus began to say of John to the crowds, Who did you come out to this desert to see? A stalk swayed by wind? But what did you come out to see? A man in loose clothes? Look, they wear loose clothes in the courts of kings. But what did you come out to see? A prophet? Yes, I tell you, and more than a prophet. This is the one of whom it is written,

> Look, I send my emissary ahead of you,
>
> who prepares the way for you.

Truly I say to you, there has not arisen from those born to woman a greater than John the baptizer, though in the realm of the sky the least is greater than him. From the days of John the baptizer to the present, the realm of the sky suffers violence and the violent assault it. All the prophets and the law prophesied John, and whether or not you accept it, he is the Elijah who was to come. Anyone with ears to hear, hear.

To what can I compare this generation? It is like children in the town square calling to others, saying,

> We played the flute for you but you didn't dance,
>> we sang a dirge but you didn't mourn.

John came neither eating nor drinking, and they said, He has a visitant. The xon of humanity came eating and drinking, and they said, Look, a glutton and a drunkard, a friend of the corrupt and errant. But wisdom is proven by its works.

When Herod listened to John, he was very perplexed, but he listened willingly. An opportune day came, when Herod on his birthday gave a banquet for his officials and his officers and the bigwigs of Galilee. When Herodias' daughter came in and danced, she pleased Herod and his guests, and the king said to the girl, Ask for whatever you want, and I'll give it to you. He swore to her, Whatever you ask for I'll give you, even if it's half my realm. She went out and consulted her mother, What should I ask for? Her mother replied, The head of John the baptizer. Immediately she returned to the king to answer him, saying, I want you to give me right now the head of John the baptizer on a plate. The king was very sorry, but having made an oath in front of his guests he didn't want to refuse her, so he immediately dispatched a bodyguard with orders to bring back John's head. The bodyguard went and beheaded John in the prison, and brought back the head on a plate and gave it to the girl, and she gave it to her mother. When John's apprentices heard, they came and got his body and laid it in the tomb.

When Jesus learned of John's detention, xe withdrew. Leaving Nazareth, xe settled in Capernaum, on the coast of the Sea of Galilee, fulfilling Isaiah's prophecy:

> Land of Zebulun and land of Naphtali,
>> by way of the sea, beyond the Jordan,
>>> alien Galilee,
> the ones confined to darkness
>> have seen a bright light,

and over those confined within death's shadow
a light has risen.

From then on, Jesus spoke out, saying Reconsider, for the realm of the sky looms. This sky will dissipate and the sky above it will dissipate. Death is not alive, nor can life die, though when you ate the dead you made death live. When you enter light, what will you do? In your wholeness you were divided. In your division, what will you do? How long will death dominate? For as long as women bear children. I tell you, wholeness fills with light, division drains into darkness.

Xe returned to Nazareth, where xe'd been raised, and on the sabbath day, as usual, went to the synagogue, and stood to read. Xe was given the scroll of the prophet Isaiah, and unrolling the scroll xe found the place at which was written,

The breath of the boss is in me,
for xe has anointed me
to bring good news to the poor.
Xe has sent me to declare detainees free,
the blind sighted.
Xe has sent me to liberate the oppressed,
and pronounce upon this age the favor of the boss.

Xe rolled up the scroll, returned it to the gabbai, and sat. All in the synagogue watched xer intently, and xe declared to them, Today in your hearing what was written is fulfilled. The word sends forth from itself streams of milk, streams of honey and oil and wine, sends down strong roots, sends out lush fruit with sweet aromas, for sustenance from generation to generation, age to age.

I recede from those who overlook me
but I brood over those who look to me.

Those who killed me died,
but I live in those who sought life in me:

I am of them, I am with them,
I speak through their mouths.

The Gospel

Those who would not join in persecuting
I have yoked together with my love.

Like the arms of spouse embracing spouse,
my yoke joins together those who join with me.

Like the wedding bed made for the united pair,
so my love awaits those who wait for me.

I was not rejected by their rejecting me,
I did not die by their killing me.

Sheol could not contain me,
death could not keep those I called to me.

I made myself into the rancidness
that brings back up all the stomach's contents.

Death vomited my torso and limbs
because it could not keep down my face.

I convened the living from among the dead
and from my living mouth I spoke to them
my living and life-giving word.

Those who had died looked to me
responding to me, Xon of the god, have mercy on us,

release us from the hold of darkness,
open the door that lets us out into light.

We see that our death has not killed you:
give us life, you who are life.

I heard their plea, and with my seal secured their souls,
making them free by making them mine.

Hearing xer teach on the sabbath in the synagogue, they were struck, and asked one another, By what right does *xe* speak this way? What wisdom does *xe* have? What great deeds do *xer* hands have power to perform? Isn't this just a carpenter, Mary's son, the brother of James and Joseph, Judas and Simon? Aren't xer sisters right here among us? They were scandalized. Jesus said to them, Nowhere is a prophet so disrespected as in that prophet's own country, among kin, at home. Whoever knows the fother and the mather will be called a sonofabitch. I have everything to say, no one to say it to. I offer you what no eye can see, no ear can hear, no hand can touch, no human mind comprehend.

But I tell you this truth: many widows lived in Israel in Elijah's day, when the skies stayed closed for three and a half years, when famine spread across the land, but to none of them was Elijah sent except to one widow in Sarepta, a tiny town in Sidon. Many with leprosy lived in Israel in Elisha's day, and none was cured except Naaman the Syrian. I separate you, one from a thousand and two from ten thousand, to join you together. The truth seeks out the wise and the reverent. Faith receives, love gives. All in the synagogue, hearing these things, grew enraged, and rose to drive xer out to the brow of the hill on which the town stood, intent on throwing xer off the cliff. Xe passed right through the middle of the mob, though, and went xer way.

From the synagogue, the five, Jesus with Simon and Andrew and James and John, went straight to the home of Simon and Andrew. But Simon's mother-in-law lay sick with a fever. When they told Jesus this, xe went to her, took her hand, and helped her to her feet. Immediately, the fever left her, and she began to wait on them. That evening after sunset they brought to xer all who were ill or visited. Soon the whole town had gathered at the door. Xe healed many who had been sick with various diseases, and drove off many visitants, which xe forbade to speak, because they recognized xer.

Early in the morning, while it was still dark, xe rose and went out, off to a solitary place to pray. Simon and the others followed xer, and when they caught up they said, Everyone is looking for you. Xe replied, Let's go to the towns nearby, so I can speak there, too; it's what I came for. And xe *did* teach, in synagogues throughout Galilee, and drove off visitants.

How did the boss live? While xe existed in flesh, after xe revealed xerself as the xon of the god, xe inhabited this world in which we live, speaking of the law of nature we call death. The xon of the god was the xon of humanity. Xe embraced both divinity and humanity, being the xon of the god in order to conquer death, and being the xon of humanity in order to restore us to fullness.

☩

Xe came again to Cana in Galilee, where xe'd made the water wine. There was an official there whose son lay sick in Capernaum. Hearing that Jesus had come back from Judea to Galilee, he went to xer and asked xer to come down and heal his son, because he was near death. Jesus said to him, Unless you people see signs and wonders, you don't believe. The official said to xer, Boss, come on, before my child dies. Jesus said to him, Go, your son will live. The man believed this word that Jesus gave him, and went. As he was going back, his slaves met him, and told him his child was alive. He asked them just when the son had begun to recover; they told him, Yesterday at one in the afternoon the fever left him. The father recognized that this was the same hour when Jesus had said to him, Go, your son will live, so he believed, and so did his whole household.

After this there was a Jewish festival and Jesus went up to Jerusalem. There is in Jerusalem by the Sheep Gate a pool called in Hebrew Bethesda, that has five porches. In these lay many who were infirm: blind, lame, paralyzed. One man there had been ill for thirty-eight years. When Jesus saw him lying there, knowing he had been there a long time xe asked him, Do you want to get well? The sick man replied, Boss, I have no one to put me into the pool when the water is stirring, and when I try by myself, someone else cuts in front of me. Jesus said to him, Stand, pick up your pallet, and walk. Immediately the man was well, and he picked up his pallet and walked.

But that day was a sabbath, so the Jews told the man who'd been healed, It's the sabbath; you're not permitted to pick up your pallet. He replied to them, The one who made me well told me, Pick up your pallet and walk. They asked him, Who's the one who told you, Pick it up and walk? The healed man couldn't say who it was, because Jesus had slipped away from the crowd that was in that place. Later Jesus found him in the temple and told him, Look, you've been cured. Don't start erring now, so nothing worse happens to you. The man went away and reported to the Jews that it was Jesus who had made him well. Because of this, the Jews persecuted Jesus, for doing such things on the sabbath. But Jesus responded to them, My fother is still working, so I'm working. Because of this, the Jews all the more sought to kill xer, because xe not only broke the sabbath but also said the god was xer own fother, thus making xerself equal with the god.

Jesus said to them, Truly, truly I tell you, the xon can do nothing by xerself, if xe has not first seen the fother do it. What xe does, the xon does the same way. The fother loves the xon and shows xer all the things xe does, and will show xer even greater works than these, to amaze you. Just as the fother raises the dead and gives them life, so the xon gives life to whomever xe chooses. The fother judges no one, but has delegated all judgment to the xon, so that all will honor the xon as they honor the fother. One who does not honor the xon does not honor the fother who sent xer. Truly, truly I tell you, the one who hears my word and believes the one who sent me has timeless life and will not come to judgment but has passed from death into life. Truly, truly I tell you, the hour is coming and is now when the dead will hear the voice of the xon of the god and those who hear will live. Just as the fother has life in xerself, so xe has given the xon to have life in xerself, and has given xer authority to pass judgment, because xe is the xon of humanity. Don't be amazed by this, because the hour is coming when all who are in tombs will hear xer voice and come out: those who have done good, to the standing up into life; those who have done ill, to the standing up into judgment. I can do nothing by myself; as I hear, I judge, and my judgment is just, because I seek not my own will but the will of the one who sent me.

Xe went down into Capernaum, a town in Galilee, and on the sabbath taught its citizens. They were struck by xer teachings, because xer word was sure. In the synagogue one man, held by the breath of a toxic visitant, shouted in a loud voice, Ha! Why us, Jesus of Nazareth? Out to ruin us? I know who you are, the god-given. Shouting it down, Jesus said, Shut up! Go away! And the visitant threw the man down but left without harming him. Everyone was amazed, and they said to one another, What word is this, that has enough authority and force to command toxic breaths and drive them out? And rumors about xer washed over the region.

Jesus roved the whole of Galilee, teaching in the synagogues and proclaiming the good news of the realm and healing all the diseases and infirmities of the people. Xer fame spread all across Syria, and they brought xer all who were ill, those with various diseases and pain, the visited, those who suffered seizures or paralysis, and xe healed them. The one who spoke the word became a path for the errant, knowledge for the ignorant, discovery for the searching, support for the unsteady, cleanliness for the corrupt. A great many followed xer, people from Galilee and Decapolis and Jerusalem and Judea and beyond the Jordan.

Seeing the crowd, xe climbed the hill and sat, xer apprentices facing xer, and opening xer mouth to teach them, xe said,

> Graceful, the poor in breath: theirs is the realm of the sky.
> Graceful, the mourners: they will be consoled.
> Graceful, the unassuming: they will inherit the whole earth.
> Graceful, the alone and chosen: they will find the realm they came from and return to.
> Graceful, those who exist before being born: what is and was also will be.
> Graceful, the hungry and thirsty for justice: they will receive satisfaction.
> Graceful, the merciful: they will be shown mercy.
> Graceful, the clean-hearted: they will see the god.
> Graceful, the peacemakers: they will be recognized by the god.
> Graceful, those punished for seeking justice: theirs is the realm of the sky.

Graceful, you yourselves when people insult you, persecute you, and tell lies about you because of me. Be content, be glad: your reward is great in the skies. People also persecuted the prophets who preceded you.

Graceful the lion made human when eaten by a human, graceless the human made lion when eaten by a lion. Graceful, the one who lived before coming to life. If you live as my apprentices and hear my words, these stones will serve you. For you five trees in paradise stand unaltered by summer or winter, with leaves that never fall. Whoever knows them will not suffer death.

You are salt from the earth, but what can make bland salt salty? It's good for nothing but to be thrown back down and walked on. You are light from the cosmos. You can't hide a city built on a hill, and you don't light a lantern to cover it with a basket, but to set it on a stand, to give its light to all in the house. Just so, let your light shine so that others, seeing your good works, will praise your fother who is in the skies. A precious thing would hardly be hidden in an equally precious container. The priceless is more securely kept in what isn't worth a dime. So it is with the soul, a priceless thing hidden in the worthless body.

Don't think I've come to nullify the law or the prophets; I've come not to nullify but to fulfill. Truly I say to you, until the sky and the land pass away, not one letter, not a comma, will pass away from the law, until everything is fulfilled. Whoever annuls even the least commandment and teaches other people it's annulled will be considered least in the realm of the sky. I tell you, if your justice is not more robust than that of the scribes and Pharisees, you will not enter the realm of the sky.

You have heard that it was commanded to the ancients, Do not murder; one who murders will be subject to judgment. I say to you that one who is angry at his sibling will be subject to judgment, one who calls his sibling Loser will be subject to the court, and one who calls his sibling Fool will be subject to the fire of Gehenna. Anger spreads fear; fear sponsors anger. So if you are laying a gift at the altar and just then remember that your sibling has something against you, drop your gift there and go; first seek reconciliation with your sibling, and then offer your gift. Come to terms with your accuser while you're on your way to court with him, so your accuser doesn't hand you to the judge, and the judge hand you to the bailiff, and you be thrown into jail. I tell you, then you won't get out until you've paid the last cent.

You have heard that it was commanded, Do not commit adultery. But I say to you that to look at another with lust is to commit adultery in your heart. If your right eye leads you astray, pluck it out and throw it away: better to lose one part than have your whole body thrown into Gehenna. If your right hand leads you astray, cut it off and throw it away. Better to lose one part than to lose your whole body to Gehenna.

Again, you have heard that it was commanded to the ancients, Do not swear falsely, but perform for the boss what you have sworn to do. I tell you, Don't swear at all, not by the sky, because it's the throne of the god, not by the earth, because it's the god's footstool, not by Jerusalem, because it's the city of the great king, and not by your head, because you don't have the power to make one hair white or black. Let your word for yes be yes, for no be no; anything else comes from the harmful one.

You have heard that it was commanded, Eye for eye and tooth for tooth. I say to you, don't retaliate against one who harms. If someone slaps you on your right cheek, turn the other to him. If someone sues you for your coat, give him your shirt, too. If someone demands that you walk one mile, walk two. Give to one who begs, and don't turn your back to one who would borrow.

You have heard that it was commanded, Love your neighbor and hate your enemy. I say to you, Love your enemies and pray for your tormentors, so that you may be a child of your fother in the skies, because xe makes the sun rise on the bad and the good, and makes rain fall on the just and the unjust. If you love those who love you, what reward are you owed? Don't even brokers do that? If you embrace your kin, what more are you doing than others? Don't even hatemongers do that? Be complete, as your fother in the skies is complete.

Take care not to perform your justice in front of others, to be seen by them; doing so you'll receive no reward from your fother in the skies. When you give to charity, don't sound a trumpet to announce it, as hypocrites do in synagogues and in the streets, to be praised by other people. Truly I tell you, they have their reward. When you give to charity, don't let your left hand know what your right hand is doing, so that you give in secrecy, and your fother who sees in secrecy will reward you.

And when you pray, don't mimic hypocrites, who love to show themselves praying in synagogues and at street corners, to be seen by others. Truly I tell you, they have their reward. When you pray, go into your room and close the door and pray to your fother who stays in secrecy, and your fother who sees in secrecy will reward you. When you pray, don't spout clichés as most people do, to be heard saying lots of words. Don't be like them; your fother knows what you need before you ask xer. Hate hypocrisy and ill will. Ill will generates hypocrisy, and hypocrisy is far from truth.

Pray like this:

> Our fother in the skies,
>> may your name be honored,
>> your rule continue,
>> your decision take place
>>> on earth just as in the sky.
> Give us today enough bread for the day.
> Forgive of our debts to you
>> as much as we forgive of others' debts to us.
> Direct us, not toward temptation
>> but away from harmfulness.

If you forgive others' offenses against you, your fother in the sky will forgive you, but if you don't forgive others, you fother won't forgive your offenses.

Similarly, when you fast, don't look dismal the way hypocrites do, showing sallow faces so others will see that they're fasting. Truly I tell you, they have their reward. But when you fast, brush your hair and wash your face, so your fasting won't be noticed by other people but by your fother who stays in secrecy, and your fother who sees in secrecy will reward you.

When you praise, praise like this:

> Hear us, fother, as you heard your only xon,
>> receiving xer to yourself, restoring xer with rest from xer
>> many works.

Your power gives off brighter light than glinting armor.
Your word invites reconsideration and offers life.
You are the clear thinking and inner calm of the solitary.
Again, hear us as you heard your chosen,
  by your sacrifice granting entry to the souls
  their good works liberated from dull bodily limbs to live
    forever.

Don't store for yourself stores on earth, where moth and rust erase, and where robbers break in and rob. Store for yourself stores in the sky, where neither moth nor rust erases, and where no robbers break in and rob. Where your store is, there too is your heart.

The lamp of the body is the eye, so if your eye is sound your whole body will be lit, but if your eye is clouded, your whole body will be darkened. If the light in you is darkness, what darkness!

As no one can mount two horses or stretch two bows, so no one can report to two bosses. Either you'd hate the one and love the other or be devoted to one and despise the other. You can't report to god and money.

Because of this I say to you, when it comes to health, don't fret what to eat, or when it comes to the body, what to wear. Isn't health more than food, isn't the body more than clothes? Look to the birds in the sky that don't plant or harvest or gather into barns, yet your fother in the sky feeds them. Don't you matter as much as they do? Which of you by worrying can add one day to your lifespan? And why worry over clothes? Look at how the lilies of the field grow: they don't labor or spin, but I tell you even Solomon in all his splendor never dressed as well as one of these. If that's how the god clothes the grass in the field, that's alive today but tomorrow burned in the oven, how well will xe clothe you, you meagerfaiths?

Don't worry, then, asking what to eat, what to drink, what to wear. Let others seek those things that your fother in the sky already knows you need. You seek first the realm of the god and xer justice, and all these will follow. Don't worry for tomorrow; let tomorrow worry for itself. Each day affords trouble enough of its own.

If you do have money, don't lend it at interest; give it to one from whom you'll never get it back. A pearl does not lose value by being dropped into mud, or gain value by being rubbed with balsam; it's always precious in its owner's eyes. Similarly, the children of the god remain precious in their fother's eyes, their circumstances notwithstanding.

Do not judge, so as not to be judged, for the judgment you judge with judges you, and the measure you measure with measures you. Why do you notice the splinter in your sibling's eye but overlook the joist in your own? And how can you say to your sibling, Let me pluck that splinter from your eye, when you have a joist in your own? Hypocrite, first dig the joist from your own eye; then you will see clearly enough to pluck the splinter from your sibling's eye. Don't offer dogs what is holy, and don't toss pearls to pigs; they'll just trample them when they turn on you.

Ask and it will be given you, seek and you will find, knock and the door will be opened to you. All who ask receive, all who seek find, all who knock enter. Who among you, if your child asks for bread will give a stone, or if for a fish will give a snake? If you who are harmful determine to give good gifts to your children, how much more surely will your fother in the skies give good gifts to those who ask xer.

In everything act toward others as you would have them act toward you: this sums the law and the prophets. Jesus said, Love your sibling as you love your soul, protect your sibling as carefully as you protect your own eyes.

Enter through the narrow gate. A wide gate and a broad road lead to destruction, and many enter there. A tight gate and a narrow road lead to life, and few find it.

Beware of false prophets. They approach you dressed as sheep, but inside they are ravenous wolves. You can recognize them by their fruit: no point looking to gather grapes from thornbushes or figs from thistles. A sound tree bears sweet fruit, but a rotting tree bears bitter fruit. A sound tree does not bear bitter fruit, nor a rotting tree sweet fruit. Every tree that does not bear sweet fruit is cut for firewood. Recognize them by their fruit.

Not everyone who addresses me as boss, boss will enter the realm of the sky, only the ones who do the will of my fother who is in the skies. When the day comes, many will plead, Boss, boss, didn't we prophesy in your name, and expel visitants in your name, and in your name make many shows of strength? But I'll reply to them, I never knew you, get away from me, you unprincipled frauds.

Anyone who listens to these principles of mine and practices them will resemble the wise person who built on bedrock, so even though rain fell and rivers rose and winds gusted against the house, it didn't fall, because it stood on rock. Anyone who hears but does not practice these principles will resemble the dolt who built on sand, and when rain fell and rivers rose and winds gusted against that house, down it tumbled.

One who knows everything except herself knows nothing. Whoever discerns the hidden meaning of these my sayings will not suffer death.

By the end of Jesus' words, the people in the crowd were amazed at xer instruction, because xe taught with xer own authority, not the way their scribes taught.

╬

Once the crowd realized that Jesus and xer apprentices were no longer there, they went to Capernaum to look for xer. When they found xer on the other shore of the sea, they said to xer, Rabbi, when did you come here? In reply, Jesus said to them, Truly, truly I tell you, you seek me not because you've seen signs, but because you ate the loaves and were filled. Don't work for the bread that goes stale but for the bread that lasts through timeless life, that the xon of humanity gives you, because it is xer that the fother has certified. They asked xer, What should we do, to work the works of the god? In answer Jesus said to them, This is the work of the god, to believe on the one xe has sent. They said to xer, What sign will you perform, so that seeing it we will believe you? What work? Our fathers ate manna in the desert, so it's written,

Xe gave them bread from the sky to eat.

Jesus said to them, Truly, truly I tell you, Moses didn't give you bread from the sky, but my fother gives you the true bread from the sky: the bread of the god is the one who comes down from the sky and gives life to the world.

They said to xer, Boss, give us this bread from now on. Jesus said to them, I am the bread of life. The one who comes to me won't hunger, and the one who believes on me will never be thirsty. But as I've told you, though you've seen, you don't believe. Everyone the fother gives to me will come to me, and those who come to me I will not turn away, because I came down from the sky not to do my own will but to do the will of the one who sent me. This is the will of the one who sent me, that of all who are given me I should lose none but raise up each one on the last day. This is the will of my fother, that everyone who sees the xon and believes on xer have timeless life, and that I raise up each one on the last day.

The Jews began to grumble about xer because xe said, I am the bread that comes down from the sky. They asked, Isn't this Jesus, the xon of Joseph, whose father and mother we know? How can xe now claim, I came down from the sky? In reply, Jesus said to them, Don't grumble among yourselves. No one can come to me, unless drawn to me by the fother who sent me, and I will raise up that person on the last day. It's written in the prophets, *And all will be taught by god.* Everyone who listens to the fother and learns will come to me. Not that anyone has seen the fother except the one who is of the god: that one has seen the fother. Truly, truly I tell you, the one who believes has timeless life. I am the bread of life. Your fathers ate manna in the desert, but they died. This is the bread that comes down from the sky, so that whoever eats from it won't die. I am the bread of life that came down from heaven. Whoever eats from this bread will live timelessly, and this bread that I give for the life of the world is my flesh.

The Jews began to argue with each other, asking, How can xe give us xer flesh to eat? Jesus said to them, Truly, truly I tell you, if you don't eat the flesh of the xon of humanity and drink xer blood, you have no life in you. The one who feeds on my flesh and drinks my blood has timeless life, and I will raise up that person on the last day. My flesh is true food, and my blood true drink. The one who feeds on my flesh and drinks my blood remains in me and I in that person. Just as the living fother sent me and I live because of the fother, so the one who feeds on me lives because of me. This is the bread that came down from the sky, not like what your fathers ate, who then died: the one who feeds on this bread will live timelessly. Xe said these things in the synagogue, teaching in Capernaum.

Many of xer apprentices, hearing this, said, This word is hard; who can hear it? Jesus, knowing the apprentices were grumbling about it, asked them, Does this disturb you? Seeker, seek until you find. Finding finds disturbance, disturbance stirs up wonder, wonder opens onto totality. What if you were to see the xon of humanity ascending to where xe was before? It's the breath that gives life; the flesh offers no profit. Don't fear the flesh, but don't love it. If you fear the flesh, it will dominate you; if you love the flesh, it will swallow you up and suffocate you. The sayings I speak to you are breath and they are life. But among you there are some who don't believe. Jesus knew from the beginning who would not believe, and which one would betray xer. Xe said, This is why I told you that no one can come to me unless it be granted by the fother.

Because of this many of xer apprentices went back where they came from and no longer traveled around with xer. So Jesus asked the twelve, Don't you want to leave, too? Simon Peter replied, Boss, to whom would we go? You have the words of timeless life, and we believe and know that you are the holy one of the god. Jesus answered them, Have I not chosen you? But one of you is a devil. Xe spoke of Judas, son of Simon Iscariot, the one who, though among the twelve, was going to betray xer.

Xe came down off the hill, followed by huge crowds, and, look, a person with leprosy approached, prostrating himself, saying to xer, Boss, if you choose to, you can cleanse me. Jesus put out xer hand and touched him, saying, I do choose, be clean. Immediately, he was cleaned of his leprosy. And Jesus said to him, See that you tell no one; for your testimony to others, just go to the priest and offer the gift Moses commanded.

When xe had entered Capernaum, a centurion approached, appealing to xer, saying, Boss, my child is lying paralyzed at home, suffering badly. Jesus said, I'll come heal him. The centurion replied, saying, Boss, I am not worthy for you to stand under my roof; only say the word, and my child will be healed. I'm a man of authority, with soldiers under my command. I say to one, Go, and he goes, and to another, Come, and he comes, and to a slave, Do this, and he does. Hearing this, Jesus was amazed, and said to those following xer, Truly I tell you, I haven't found such faith in anyone from Israel. I tell you, many will come, from east and west, and dine with Abraham, Isaac, and Jacob in the realm of the sky, but the children of this realm will be expelled into outer darkness, where there will be weeping and grinding of teeth. To the centurion, Jesus said, Go; it will happen just as you believed. And at that very moment the child was healed. Jesus said: The one who is old enough in days to ask unhesitatingly a seven-day-old child about the place of life will live, for the first and the last will prove one and the same.

On the evening of the same day xe said to them, Let's cross to the other side. So they sent away the crowd, and set out with xer aboard, and accompanied by other boats. A fierce storm arose, with waves breaking over the boat, filling it fast. Jesus lay in the stern, sleeping on a mat, but they woke xer, saying, Teacher, don't you care if we drown? So xe arose and rebuked the wind and ordered the sea, Peace, be still. The wind died down to perfect calm. Xe said to them, Why such cowardice? Have you no faith? But they feared fearfully, and wondered to one another, Who is this, that even wind and waves obey xer?

They crossed to the other side of the sea, to the region of the Gerasenes. Jesus had barely left the boat when from among the tombs a man with a toxic breath confronted xer. He lived among the tombs, and even with chains no one could keep him restrained: when they'd bound him hand and foot, he simply broke the chains. No one could subdue him. All night, all day, among the tombs and in the hills he would wail and gnash himself with stones. But seeing Jesus from a long way off, he ran to xer and bowed down, and loudly shouted, What am I to you, Jesus, xon of the highest god? By that god I beg you don't torment me. Jesus first commanded, Leave this man, you toxic breath. Then he demanded, What's your name? It answered, My name is Legion, for we are many. It begged xer not to send it out of the region.

On one of the hills a herd of pigs was feeding, so the breaths begged Jesus, Send us into the pigs; let us enter them. Xe gave them permission, and departing the man they entered the pigs. The herd, all two thousand pigs, stampeded down the hillside into the sea and drowned. The swineherds ran off, and told people everywhere, and all came out to see what had happened. They found Jesus, and saw beside xer the man who had been visited, sitting, dressed and sane, and they were afraid. The ones who had witnessed it repeated the story of the visitants and the pigs, and the people asked Jesus to leave their region. As Jesus was getting into the boat, the man who'd been visited asked to join xer, but Jesus said, Go home to your people and report to them what the boss has done for you and how xe has had mercy on you. So the man left and proclaimed in Decapolis what Jesus had done for him, and everyone was amazed.

As they were walking along the road, someone said to xer, I'll follow you wherever you go. Jesus replied, Foxes have dens and birds of the sky have nests, but the xon of humanity has nowhere to rest xer head. To another, xe said, Follow me, but that one replied, Let me first go bury my father. Xe said to him, Let the dead bury their dead; you go out and proclaim the realm of the god. Yet another person said, Boss, I will follow you, just let me go and say goodbye to my household. But Jesus said, No one who puts hand to plow but then looks back is fit for the realm of the god. My followers haven't followed me. Unless you lose the world, you will not find the realm; unless you take a sabbath from the sabbath, you will not see the fother. One who comprehends the cosmos has caught a corpse; to one who has caught a corpse the cosmos can't compare.

Xe returned to Capernaum, and it got around that xe was back home. So many gathered that there was no way to get to the door to hear xer intoning the word. One group came, bringing a person who was paralyzed, carried by four of them. Unable to squeeze through the crowd, they took to the roof, creating an opening through which they let the stretcher down. When Jesus saw their faith, xe said to the patient, Child, your errors are removed from you. Some scribes sitting there thought to themselves, How can xe speak that way? Xe's blaspheming. Who has power to remove error, except the god? Immediately, sensing within xerself what they were thinking, Jesus said to them, Why think to yourself in this way? Which is easier, to say to a paralyzed person Your errors are removed, or to say, Stand, pick up your stretcher, and walk around? I'll show you that the xon of humanity has authority to dismiss errors. Xe said then to the paralyzed person, I say to you, Stand, pick up your stretcher, and go to your own home. And he stood, and immediately picked up his stretcher and started off, right in front of everyone, so they were all amazed and praised the god, saying, We've never seen anything like this.

As Jesus was walking on from there, xe saw a man named Matthew sitting in the broker's office, and xe said to him, Follow me. And Matthew rose and followed xer. It happened that while xe was reclining at Matthew's table, many brokers and crooks came and ate with Jesus and xer apprentices. Seeing this, the Pharisees said to xer apprentices, Why does your teacher eat with brokers and crooks? Hearing this, xe replied, It's not the well who need a doctor, it's the ill. Go figure out what this means: *I favor mercy over sacrifice.* I have come to call not the just but the crooked. The principals attempt to deceive the people, recognizing the people's kinship with the truly good. They take the names of good things and assign them to bad things, to deceive the people, affiliating them by the names with bad things, as if it were doing the people a favor to consider bad things good. In this way, they transform free people into slaves forever.

The apprentices of John and the Pharisees were fasting, and some people came and questioned xer: Why do the apprentices of John and the apprentices of the Pharisees fast, but your apprentices don't fast? Jesus answered them, Do wedding guests fast while the groom is present? When they're with the groom, it wouldn't do to fast. The time will come when the groom is taken from them, and on that day they can fast.

No one sews a piece of unshrunk cloth onto an old shirt: the patch would only tear away and leave the hole bigger than before. And no one pours new wine into old wineskins: it would only burst the skins and spill the wine. New wine goes in fresh skins. Glass vases and ceramic pitchers both are made with fire, but if glass vases break they can be remade, because they were shaped by breath. Ceramic pitchers that break, though, are discarded, because they were shaped without breath. Whoever drinks from my mouth will become like me. I will become that person, and the hidden things will be revealed to that person.

When Jesus had crossed by boat back to the other side, a large crowd gathered around xer, right there at the shore. One of the leaders of the synagogue, named Jairus, came and, seeing xer, fell at xer feet. Pleading to xer, he said, My little daughter is at the point of death; come lay your hands on her, so that she'll be healed, and live. And Jesus went with him.

A large crowd followed, pressing on xer, and a woman who'd been having hemorrhages for twelve years and suffered greatly and spent all she had on doctors, though her condition got worse instead of better, having heard of Jesus, pushed through the crowd behind xer and touched xer cloak, because she'd told herself, If only I can touch xer cloak, I'll be cured. Immediately her hemorrhaging stopped, and in her body she sensed the curing of her illness. But immediately Jesus, in xerself sensing the power drawn out, turned to the crowd and demanded, Who touched my cloak? Xer apprentices said, You see how thick this crowd is, and you ask who touched your cloak? But xe looked around to see who had done it. The woman, trembling from fear, knowing what had happened in her, came and fell down before xer and told xer the whole truth. Xe said to her, Daughter, your faith has healed you. Go in peace, cured of your illness.

Even as xe was speaking, people came from the synagogue leader's house, saying, Your daughter has died; why trouble the teacher now? But Jesus, disregarding their report, said to the synagogue leader, Don't fear; have faith. Xe allowed no one to follow xer except Peter and James and John the brother of James. When they reached the house of the synagogue leader, Jesus saw the commotion, people weeping and wailing loudly, but going inside xe said, Why this commotion and weeping? The girl is not dead, only sleeping. They laughed at xer, but, shooing them out, xe took the girl's mother and father and the ones who were with xer and went in where the girl was lying. Xe took the girl's hand and said to her,

Talitha koum, which translates to Girl, I tell you to rise. Immediately the girl stood up and began to walk around. She was twelve years old. They were astonished beyond astonishment. Xe instructed that no one should know about this, and told them to give her something to eat.

As Jesus was leaving, two blind persons followed xer, crying out, saying, Show us mercy, xon of David. When xe got to the house, the blind persons approached xer and Jesus said to them, Do you believe I'm able to do this? They said to xer, Yes, boss. Then xe touched their eyes, saying to them, Let it happen to you according to your faith. Their eyes opened. Jesus gave them strict instructions, See that no one knows. But when they left, they spread news of xer across the land.

As they were leaving, a visited man who could not speak was brought to xer. Once the visitant had been expelled the man spoke, and the crowds marveled, saying, Nothing like this have ever shown itself in Israel. But the Pharisees said, xe expels visitants by the principal of visitants.

Jesus wandered the cities and towns, teaching in their synagogues and proclaiming the good news of the realm, healing all diseases and all infirmities. Xe said to xer apprentices, The harvest is bountiful but the workers few. Pray that the boss of the harvest will assign workers to the harvest. Farming in this world depends on four essentials. A harvest can be gathered into the barn only through the work of water, earth, air, and light. Similarly, the god's farming depends on four essentials: faith, hope, love, and knowledge. Faith is the earth in which we take root, hope the water by which we receive sustenance, love the air in which we grow, knowledge the light by which we ripen.

And calling xer twelve apprentices to xer, xe gave them authority over toxic breaths, to expel them, and to heal all diseases and all infirmities. Here are the names of the twelve envoys: first Simon, who is called Peter, and his brother Andrew; James the son of Zebedee and his brother John; Philip and Bartholomew; Thomas and the broker

Matthew; James the son of Alphaeus, and Thaddaeus; Simon the Cananean; and Judas Iscariot, who betrayed Jesus.

Jesus assigned the twelve, and charged them, saying, Don't travel the way of others, don't enter any city of Samaritans, but instead go to the lost sheep of the house of Israel, and as you go, speak out, declaring that the realm of the sky looms. Heal the sick, raise the dead, cure the leprous, expel visitants. Freely you have received; freely give. Carry no gold or silver or copper in your pockets. No bag, not two cloaks, no shoes, no walking stick. Workers deserve their keep. In any city or town you enter, ask who in it is worthy, and stay with them until you leave. As you enter the house, greet it with peace. If it is worthy, it will embrace your peace; if not, preserve the peace returned to you. When anyone refuses to receive you or hear you, as you leave that house or city swipe its dust off your feet. Truly I tell you, it will be more tolerable for Sodom and Gomorrah on the day of trial than for that city. I will carry you on my shoulders. Return the way you departed. Avoid beasts. The burden you have been bearing will no longer be your burden. Bring something from every house into the house of the fother, but don't take anything away from the house of the fother. When you find someone who was not given birth by a woman, fall to your face and worship xer: xe is your fother.

Look, I send you out as sheep among wolves, so be savvy as snakes but harmless as doves. Beware of humans: they will turn you in to their councils and whip you in their places of worship. And you will be brought up before governors and kings, made an example of to them and to others. But when they turn you in, don't worry over how to speak or what to say: it will be given you in the moment what to say, because it won't be you speaking but the breath of your fother speaking through you. Truly I tell you, the living god lives in you as you live in the living god. Brother will turn in brother to death, and father turn in child, and children rebel against parents and have them put to death, and you will be hated by all because of my name, but one who stands to the end will be preserved. When they persecute you in this city, migrate to that. Truly I tell you, you will not cover the cities of Israel before the arrival of the xon of humanity.

Jesus said, If they ask you, Where have you come from?, answer them, We came from the light, from the source where light generates itself, illuminating their image. If they ask you, Are you it?, answer them, We are its children, the chosen of the living fother. If they ask you, What feature proves you're from the fother?, answer them, Motion in rest. Student is not over teacher, nor slave over boss. Enough that the student model the teacher, the slave model the master. If they call the head of the household Beelzebul, what will they not call others in the household?

So do not fear them. Nothing covered up will not be discovered; nothing concealed will not be known. Most beings in this world live only on condition that their innards remain hidden: if the innards are exposed, the being dies. This is true of human beings: as long as a person's intestines remain hidden, the person can live, but anyone whose intestines are exposed dies. Same for a tree: while its roots are hidden, the tree grows and leafs out, but if the roots are exposed, the tree withers. What was hidden from you will become visible to you when you recognize what is right in front of you. Nothing obscure cannot be made plain. What I tell you in darkness, speak in the light; what you hear into your ear, from the housetops. Don't fear murderers of the body, who can't kill the soul; fear the one who can undo body and soul in Gehenna. Miserable the body that depends on body, and miserable the soul that depends on them both. Aren't sparrows sold two for a buck? Yet not one falls to the ground apart from your fother. Even the hairs on your head are numbered. Don't fear: you are valued by yourself more than sparrows by the flock.

All who commend me to humans, I will commend to my fother in the skies, but all who deny me to humans, I will deny to my fother in the skies. The slave seeks freedom, not the shareholder's estate. The xon, not only a xon, inherits from the fother. Heirs to the dead are dead, and inherit death. Heirs to the living are alive, and inherit both life and death. The dead inherit nothing: how could death inherit? If the dead inherited life, the living would not die, and the dead would return to life.

Don't think I've come to bring peace to the earth: I have come to bring not peace but a sword. I have come to divide

a man from his father
> and a daughter from her mother
and a daughter-in-law from her mother-in-law:
> family members, enemies.

One who loves father or mother more than me is not worthy of me, and one who loves son or daughter more than me is not worthy of me. One who secures his soul for himself forfeits it, and one who forfeits his soul to me secures it for himself. Death and life are offered everyone; the one they want, they choose.

One who receives you receives me, and one who receives me receives the one who sent me. One who receives a prophet will be granted a prophet's reward, and one who receives a just person will be granted a just person's reward. One who even gives a cup of cold water to one of the belittled in the name of an apprentice, truly I tell you, that giver will not go unrecompensed.

And it happened that when Jesus finished this charge to xer twelve apprentices, xe went on from there to teach and proclaim in all their cities.

Then xe began to censure the cities in which most of xer acts of power had been performed, because they did not reconsider. Oh you, Chorazin, oh you, Bethsaida, if the acts of power that were performed in you had been performed in Tyre and Sidon, they'd have reconsidered by now with sackcloth and ashes. I tell you, on the day of trial it will be better for Tyre and Sidon than for you. And you, Capernaum,

> will you be raised up to the sky?

> No, you will descend to Hades.

If the acts of power that were performed in you had been performed in Sodom, it would still stand today. I tell you, on the day of trial it will be more bearable for Sodom than for you.

Then the preserver, continuing, declared, Oh you, godless ones, your vain hopes depend on what cannot last.

Oh you, who hope in the flesh, that prison of the perishing. How long will you be oblivious, assuming that the imperishable will perish? By resting your hope on the world, taking this life as your god, you are corrupting your souls.

Oh you, burned by the insatiable fire that burns in you.

Oh you, spun by the wheel that spins in your mind.

Oh you, singed by the smoldering in you: it will devour your flesh openly, tear your souls secretly, and make you indistinguishable from one another.

Oh you, captives, kept in caves. You laugh, giddy with mad laughter, not recognizing your ruination, attentive to your plight, not understanding that you dwell in darkness and death. Instead, you are drunk with fire and rank with bile. Your hearts are so frenzied by the burning within you that you taste as sweet the poison of your enemies. Darkness rather than light rises within you, and you have surrendered your freedom to slavery. You have hidden away your hearts, and given over your minds to stupidity. Smoke from the fire within you has darkened your hearts, its dark cloud dimming your light. You dress in unclean clothes and hold to vain hopes. You believe contrary to what is known. In your detention you pretend to freedom. You've drowned your souls in dark water. You've succumbed to your impulses.

Oh you, given over to error, inattentive to the sunlight that looks down on the world and illuminates the world, disclosing the movements of the enemy. You don't even notice the moon, looking down night and day, washing the bodies of your genocides.

The god is a human-eater. Humans must be sacrificed to the god. Back when animals were sacrificed, what they were sacrificed to were hardly gods. The world is a corpse-eater. Everything that dies in it gets eaten. Truth is a life-eater, so one nourished by truth will not die. I came from the realm of truth, and those sustained by the food I brought from there will not die. Where there are three gods, they are godly; where there are two or one, I am with that one.

Matthew said to xer, Boss, no one can discern truth except through you. Teach us truth. The preserver said, What is is infinite, incomprehensible, imperishable, singular, uniformly good, flawless, timeless, graceful, unknown but self-knowing, immeasurable, unrepresentable, perfect, spotless, blessed and blessing, called the fother of it all. Anyone with ears to hear about infinite things, hear. I speak to those who are awake. Xe continued, The perishable perishes, because it comes from perishing; the imperishable does not perish, because it embraces imperishability. Humans err when they don't recognize this difference.

At that point, xe continued by saying, I attest to you, fother, boss of the sky and the earth, because you have hidden these things from the wise and the learned, and revealed them to the naive. Yes, fother, let it be just as you will. All things are given over to me by my fother, and no one knows the xon except the fother, and no one knows the fother except the xon and those to whom the xon wills to reveal xer. How could one who doesn't know the xon know the fother? Look, fother, sought by evil over the earth your breath strays. It tries to flee, but can't quite shake, bitter chaos. By your grace send me, fother. Carrying the seals I will descend, I will pass through all the ages, disclose all mysteries, reveal the forms of the gods. Invoking knowledge, I will give out the secrets of the holy way.

Come to me, all who are worn out and weighed down, and I will spell you. Fit my yoke to yourself and learn from me, because I am mild and humble in heart, and you will find rest for your souls, because my yoke is snug and my load is light. I am the hope of the hopeless, the help of the helpless, the wealth of the poor, the health of the sick, the life of the dead. Through the weak I weakened, through the hungry I hungered, through the thirsty I thirsted.

It happened that on the sabbath xe was going through a grainfield, and xer apprentices as they made their way plucked a few kernels of grain. The Pharisees said to xer, Look, why are they doing what is prohibited on the sabbath? Xe replied, Have you never read what David did when he and those with him were hungry and out of food? How he went into the house of the god, while Abiathar was high priest, and ate the offering loaves that it is forbidden for anyone but priests to eat, and shared them with the others? Jesus continued, The sabbath exists for humans, not humans for the sabbath, so the xon of humanity is boss over the sabbath.

It happened that on another sabbath xe went into the synagogue and taught. There was a man there whose right hand was withered. He said to Jesus, I was a mason, earning my living with my hands; please restore my health to me, so that I need not beg for my food.

The scribes and Pharisees watched xer to see if xe would heal on the sabbath, so they would have an accusation against xer. But xe knew what they were thinking, so xe said to the man with the withered hand, Come, stand front and center. The man stood. Jesus said to them, Which is forbidden on the sabbath, to do good or to do ill? To preserve life or to end it? Xe looked around at them all, then said to him, Extend your hand. He did, and his hand was restored. They were full of rage, and plotted among one another what to do to Jesus.

But Jesus with xer apprentices withdrew to the sea, and a large crowd followed, from Galilee and from Judea and from Jerusalem and Idumea and beyond the Jordan and from Tyre and Sidon, a large crowd that, having heard of xer deeds, came to xer. Xe told xer apprentices to keep a small boat ready so that the press of the crowd would not crush xer. Xe had healed so many that all who suffered affliction and disease kept trying to touch xer. And toxic breaths, when they recognized xer, fell down before xer and loudly shouted, You are the xon of the god. And xe strictly instructed them not to identify xer.

Next xe traveled to the town called Nain, and xer apprentices and many other people traveled with xer. But as xe neared the city gate, a dead man was being carried out. He was his mother's only son, and she was a widow. Many people from the town were with her. When xe saw her, the boss, sympathizing with her, said to her, Don't cry. Xe approached and touched the bier, and the pallbearers stopped. Xe said, Young man, I say to you, get up. The dead man sat up, and Jesus gave the man back to his mother. Fear gripped everyone there, and they praised the god, saying, A great prophet has arisen among us, and the god is protecting xer people. Word of Jesus spread across Judea, and all around.

One of the Pharisees invited Jesus to eat with him, so xe entered the Pharisee's home and reclined for the meal, and, look, an errant woman from that city, when she learned that Jesus was in the Pharisee's home, brought an alabaster jar of oil and knelt behind xer at xer feet weeping, and began to wet xer feet with her tears. She wiped them with her hair and kissed them and treated them with the oil. Seeing this, the Pharisee who had invited xer said to himself, if xe were a prophet, xe would know who is touching xer, what kind of woman she is, that she's an errant. Jesus responded, Simon, I have something to say. He replied, Tell me, teacher. Jesus said, A lender had two borrowers: one owed him five hundred dollars, the other fifty. Neither was able to pay, so he forgave both debts. Which of the two will love him more? Simon replied, I guess the one who was forgiven more. Xe replied, You've judged correctly. Turning toward the woman, xe said to Simon, See this woman? When I came into your house, you offered me no water for my feet, but she has wet them with her tears and wiped them with her hair. You gave me no kiss, but from the moment she arrived she hasn't stopped kissing my feet. Because the perfect conceive and give birth by kissing, we too kiss, to conceive of one another in grace. You poured nothing on my head, but she has treated my feet with oil. I tell you, her many errors are forgiven, and she returns much love; the one forgiven less loves less. To her, xe said, Your errors are forgiven. Those reclining at the meal muttered to one another, Who is xe, to forgive errors? Xe said to the woman, Your faith has preserved you; go in peace.

Afterward, xe traveled to cities and towns, declaring the good news of the realm of the god. The twelve were with xer, and so were certain women who had been healed of harmful breaths and debilities, Mary who was called Magdalene, from whom seven visitants had been expelled, Joanna the wife of Herod's steward Chuza, Susanna, and many others, each with her own resourcefulness advancing xer ministry. Three were ever watching over the boss: Mary xer mother, Mary xer sister, Mary Magdalene, who is called xer beloved. Mary names xer mother, xer sister, xer beloved.

The preserver's beloved was Mary Magdalene. Xe loved her more than xe loved the other apprentices, and xe often kissed her on the mouth. The other apprentices complained to xer, Why do you love her more than you love us? In answer, the preserver said, Why don't I love you like I love her? When a person who can see and one who cannot stand together in darkness they resemble one another, but when light comes out the one who can see sees what is lit, but the one who cannot remains in darkness. Simon Peter said to them, Let's make Mary leave us, since females aren't up to this life. Jesus said, I myself will trans her, to make her male, so that her living breath matches that of any male. Every female who makes herself thus male will enter the realm of the sky.

Gathering them around xer, xe spoke to them in parables. How can Satan expel Satan? If a realm is divided against itself, that realm cannot stand, and if a house is divided against itself, that house cannot stand. If Satan rebels against himself and is divided, he cannot stand but meets his end. No one, having entered a strong person's house, can steal the person's property without first tying him up, *then* setting about to steal. Truly I tell you, all errors will be forgiven the children of humans, and all the blasphemies they blaspheme, except that one who blasphemes against the holy breath will never have forgiveness, but will always carry the liability of that error. That, because they'd been saying, xe has a toxic breath.

While the crowd was still growing, xe began to speak. This generation is a harmful generation; it seeks a sign, but will be given no sign except the sign of Jonah. As Jonah was a sign to the people of Nineveh, so will the xon of humanity be for this generation. The queen of the south will rise against the people of this generation in the trial and condemn them, because she came from the ends of the earth to hear the wisdom of Solomon, but, look, here is something greater than Solomon. The people of Nineveh will rise against the people of this generation in the trial and condemn them, because at the warning of Jonah they reconsidered, but, look, here is something greater than Jonah.

Names assigned to things of this world deceive, turning the heart away from the perfect to the imperfect. One who hears the word *god* conceives not the perfect but the imperfect. Similarly, with *fother*, *xon*, *holy breath*, *life*, *light*, *resurrection*, *church*, and all the rest, people conceive not the perfect but the imperfect, unless they know the perfect. Names heard in the world deceive. Names from the timeless realm are never uttered in this world, and don't designate things in this world, but refer instead to what is of the timeless realm.

When a toxic breath goes out of someone, it wanders waterless regions seeking rest, but, finding none, it says, I'll go back to the house I left. Arriving, it finds the place swept and tidied. So it goes and gathers seven other breaths more destructive than itself. They enter and live there, and the later condition of the person proves worse than the earlier.

Xer mother and xer brothers came to see xer, but could not get near because of the crowd. Xe was told, Your mother and brothers are standing outside, wanting to see you. But xe replied, My mather and my siblings are those who listen to and perform the word of the god. Just now my mather, the holy breath, lifting me by one hair, transported me to the top of Mt. Tabor. I am in the breath and truth of matherhood, in its unity, as I am with those united in lasting friendship, who know no spite or harmfulness, but are united by my knowledge in word and peace, existing in completion with one another and in one another. Those who embrace my example embrace my word, basking forever in light, in friendship, sharing breath, in unhindered, unqualified knowledge that the one who is is one, and all are one. They have been taught by the one to be one with one another. The fother of everything is immeasurable and immutable, mind, word, division, jealousy, fire, yet wholly one, alling them all as a single principle, breathing them all with one breath.

The one is unity with nothing over it. It is the god, the parent of everything, the invisible one that is over everything, the incorruptible, pure light into which no eye can gaze, the invisible breath it's wrong to think of as a god. It is more than any god, with nothing except it to exceed it. It does not exist in some medium other than itself, since everything exists in it, and it made itself. It cannot end, because it does not need. It is wholly whole, repletion that needs nothing else to be complete, the need-not-be-lit light.

The one is illimitable, with nothing before it to limit it; unfathomable, with nothing before it to fathom it; immeasurable, with nothing before it to measure it; invisible, with nothing not it to see it; timeless, in and as timelessness; ineffable, with nothing to comprehend it or speak of it; unnamable, with nothing before it to name it.

The one is more pure, holy, and clean than light, unspeakable incorruptible, not only perfect and graceful and divine, but even more than that. The one is neither embodied nor disembodied, neither vast nor minute. It is impossible to say how *much* it is, or what *kind*. No human can understand it.

The one is not a being among beings, not *merely* superior to other beings, but so exclusively itself that it is ageless and timeless. The one is timelessness-giving timelessness, life-giving life, gracefulness-giving gracefulness, knowledge-giving knowledge, goodness-giving goodness, mercy- and redemption-giving mercy, grace-giving grace. The one *gives* without needing to *have*.

How could I describe it to you? Its realm is incorruptible, at peace, silent, restful, undisturbed, the realm of all realms, sustaining them with its goodness. We could understand nothing of this more-than-everything, were it not for the one who represents it.

╬

At the sea, xe began to teach, and so great a crowd gathered that xe boarded a boat that sat in the shallows, and the whole crowd was around it, on the shore. Xe taught them much, in parables, and in this teaching xe said, Listen. Once a sower went out to sow, and as he sowed it happened that some seed fell along the road and birds came and ate it. Some fell on rocky ground without much topsoil, and sprouted quickly in such shallow soil, but once the sun rose it got scorched and, without roots, it withered. Some fell among thistles that as they grew choked it out, and it gave no grain. Some fell onto rich soil, and did give grain, growing and spreading, and yielding thirty, sixty, even a hundred times what was sown. And xe said, Anyone with ears to hear, hear.

When the crowds had left, those who were around xer with the twelve asked about the parable, and xe said to them, To you has been given the mystery of the realm of the god, but to others everything is given in parables, so that

> Looking, they may look but not see,
>
> and listening, they may listen but not hear;
>
> otherwise, they might turn and be relieved of it.

And xe said to them, If you don't get this parable, how will you get any parable? The sower sows the word. Some people are like the seed along the road, and when the word is sown there they listen, but the satan comes immediately and snatches away the word sown in them. Some, like what is sown on rocky ground, listening to the word receive it gladly, but they're rootless and don't last long; as soon as trouble or persecution happens because of the word they stumble. Some, like seed sown among thistles, listen to the word, but the worries of the moment and the lure of wealth and the desire for more stuff intrude, choking the word so it yields no grain. And some are like what was sown on good soil; they listen to the word and accept it and yield grain thirty, sixty, a hundred times what was sown.

Xe said, That's how it is with the realm of the god: as if a person were to toss seed on the ground, and sleep and rise night and day, and the seed sprout and grow, though the person knows not how. For the earth produces grain on its own: first the stalk, then the head, then the mature seed in the head. Once the grain ripens, the person applies the sickle, because harvest has arrived.

And xe said, How compare the realm of the god? By what parable reveal it? It's like a mustard seed: smallest of the seeds we plant in the soil, but once planted it grows into the largest herb, spreading such broad leaves that birds from the sky can nest in its shade.

Jesus said, The realm of the fother resembles a woman carrying a jar full of meal. While she was walking, still a long way from home, the handle broke off and the meal spilled out behind her along the road. She didn't realize it, not having noticed anything wrong, but when she arrived hom and set down the jar, she found it empty.

The realm of the sky is like an ear of wheat that sprouted in a field, and when it ripened it scattered its seed and filled the field with ears of wheat for the next season. As for you, be sure to reap the wheat, so you may have life and be filled with the realm.

Jesus said, The realm of the fother resembles a man who wanted to assassinate someone much more powerful than himself. He practiced at home, drawing his sword and jabbing it into the wall, before he killed the powerful man.

Again, the realm of the sky is like a net that, cast into the sea, catches all kinds of fish. Once the net is drawn ashore, the fishers gather good fish into buckets, and toss back worthless ones. So will it be at the end of the age: the emissaries will go out and separate the harmful from the just, and toss them into the furnace of fire, where there will be weeping and grinding of teeth.

Xe lilted yet another parable to them: The realm of the sky is like leaven a woman mixes into meal, a few pinches plenty for the whole.

All these things Jesus said to the crowd in parables, and xe said nothing to them except in parables, to fulfill what the prophet foretold:

> I will open my mouth in parables,
>> releasing what was hidden under the foundation.

The envoys, gathering around Jesus, reported to xer all of what they'd done and taught. Xe said to them, Let's go, just us, to some deserted spot and rest a little. There'd been so many people coming and going they hadn't had time even to eat. Boarding a boat, they took off by themselves for a deserted spot, but people saw them leaving and many recognized them and went on foot from all the surrounding towns and got there first. Getting out of the boat, seeing so many people, xe felt compassion for them, because they resembled sheep without a shepherd, and xe began to teach them many things. After it was already late, xer apprentices approached xer and said, This is a deserted spot and it's already late; send them off, so they can go into the surrounding towns and villages to buy themselves something to eat. Xe replied to them, Give them something to to eat, and they asked xer, What, go buy two hundred bucks' worth of bread for them to eat? Xe asked them, How many loaves do you have? Go check. When they'd confirmed, they said, Five loaves, plus two fish. Xe instructed them to seat everyone cluster by cluster across the green grass, and the people sat group by group of fifty or a hundred. Taking the five loaves and two fish, xe looked up at the sky and blessed the loaves and broke them and gave them to xer apprentices to distribute, and xe divided the fish among everyone. They all ate their fill, and still there were twelve baskets full of chunks of bread and fish. The number who had eaten from the loaves was five thousand.

Immediately xe had xer apprentices board the boat to go back across before xer to Bethsaida, while xe sent away the crowd. Having sent them off, xe headed up the hill to pray. When night fell, the boat was out on the water, and xe alone was on land. Xe saw them struggle in their rowing because the wind was against them. In the middle of the night, xe approached them, walking on the water, and would have walked past them, but they saw xer walking on the sea and thought it was a ghost, and cried out. They all saw xer and were terrified. Immediately xe spoke to them, saying, Calm down, it's me, don't be afraid. Xe got on board the boat with them and the wind stopped, and they were completely astonished. They hadn't caught on from the incident of the loaves, because their hearts had been hardened.

Crossing over, they came to Gennesaret, and put to shore. Even while they were getting out of the boat, people recognized xer and came from all around carrying sick people on mats to wherever they heard xe was. Wherever xe went, villages or towns or farms, they laid their sick at the gathering places and begged xer to let them merely touch the hem of xer cloak, and all who touched it were healed.

Gathering together around xer, the Pharisees and certain scribes who came from Jerusalem saw that some of xer apprentices ate with base (that is, unwashed) hands. The Pharisees and all the Jews do not eat without first thoroughly washing their hands, observing the tradition of the elders, and they eat nothing from the market without first washing it, and they observe many related traditions, the washing of cups and pots and copper kettles. The Pharisees and scribes pressed xer, Why do your apprentices not walk the path of the elders, but eat their bread with base hands? Xe said to them, Isaiah beautifully prophesied of you hypocrites in what is written:

> These people honor me with their lips,
>   but in their hearts they keep their distance from me.
> They worship me falsely,
>   teaching as teachings the dictates of humans.

You eschew the command of the god, to observe the tradition of humans. And xe continued, saying to them, You completely reject the command of the god, to stick to your own tradition. Moses said, Honor your father and your mother, and, Whoever insults his father and mother accomplishes his own death. You say, If a man says to his father and mother, support from me is Corban (that is, gift), you free him to do nothing more for his father and mother. You nullify the word of the god through the tradition you pass down. And you commit many such frauds.

Calling the crowd to xer again, xe said to them, Hear me, all of you, and understand. Nothing that enters a person from outside can corrupt that person, but what comes out from within the person corrupts. Anyone with ears to hear, hear. When xe had gone into the house, away from the crowd, xer apprentices asked about the parable. Xe said to them, Are you equally ignorant? Do you not get it, that what comes into a person from outside cannot corrupt the person, because it enters not his heart but his belly, and passes through to the sewer, all food equally clean? And xe said, What comes out of a person makes the person base. From within a person's heart come ill thoughts, perversions, thefts, murders, rapes, greed, malice, deceit, sensuality, envy, blasphemy, prided, foolishness. All these things come from within, and corrupt the person. What is within you will give you life when you give it life. What is not within you has killed you already. Unify interior and exterior.

Xer apprentices asked xer, Do you want us to fast? How should we pray? Should we donate to charity? What diet should we follow? Jesus said, Don't lie, and don't do what you hate; everything is open to the sky. Nothing hidden will not be revealed, and nothing covered up will not be uncovered. If you fast, you will lead yourself into error. If you pray, you will call down on yourself condemnation. If you donate to charity, you will empty your breath. When you go to a region and walk its neighborhoods, if its people receive you, eat what they serve you, and heal their sick.

At times of destruction, when the powers bound to darkness threaten you, don't say in fear, Look, the time has come. Understand that fear is one of the weapons of the principals. Fear gives power to darkness. If you fear what looms over you, it will swallow you.

None of the subjects of darkness will spare you or show you mercy. Instead, look within, where words connect you to the earth. Over this position there can be no tyranny, no tyrant.

Xe gave that day this blessing: May what unites perfection and holy breath in light also unite the emissaries and us, the lit.

╬

Departing from there, xe went to the coast of Tyre, and entered a house wanting no one to know, but xe couldn't hide. A woman whose daughter had a toxic breath, hearing about xer, came and fell at xer feet. The woman was Greek, by birth Syrophoenician, and she begged xer to expel the visitant from her daughter. Xe said to her, Let children be fed first, because it isn't well to take bread from children and toss it to dogs. In reply, she said to xer, Boss, dogs under the table eat the children's scraps. And xe said to her, Because of this word, go your way: the visitant has gone out of your daughter. Returning to her house, she found the child asleep in bed, and the visitant expelled.

Again leaving the coast of Tyre xe passed through Sidon to the Sea of Galilee through the middle of the coasts of Decapolis. They brought to xer a person who was unable to hear or speak, entreating xer to put xer hand on him. Xe took him apart from the crowd and put xer fingers into the person's ears, and touched some of xer saliva to the person's tongue. Looking up to the sky, xe sighed and said to him, Ephphatha (that is, open up), and immediately his ears were opened and his tonguelace loosened, and he spoke plainly. Xe instructed them to tell no one, but the more xe forbade them, the more widely they spread the story. They were utterly astonished, saying, xe does everything well, xe makes the deaf hear, and the unspeaking speak.

The Pharisees came and began to argue with xer, demanding from xer a sign from the sky, to test xer. Heaving a sigh, xe said to them, Why does this generation demand a sign? Truly I tell you, no sign will be given to this generation. Why be mesmerized by evidences when I've willed you an inheritance the whole world couldn't hold?

It's impossible to see anything real without becoming like it. It's otherwise for humans in this world, who see the sun without becoming the sun, and see the sky and the earth and everything else without becoming them. But in the realm of truth, what you see, you become. You see the breath, you become breath. You see the salve, you become salve. You see the fother, you become fother. Here, you see everything except yourself. There, you see yourself, and are what you see.

Xe went to Bethsaida, and they brought to xer a blind man, begging Jesus to touch him. Xe took the blind man by the hand and led him out of the town, and when xe had spit onto his eyes and put xer hands on him, xe asked, What do you see? Looking around, he said, I see humans that look like walking trees. So again Jesus put xer hands over the man's eyes, and the man looked carefully and saw everything clearly. And xe sent him away to his own house, saying, Don't go into the town or tell anyone.

Jesus and xer apprentices went out through the towns of Caesarea Philippi, and along the way xe asked xer apprentices, Who do the people say I am? They answered, some say John the baptizer, some Elijah, some another of the prophets. Xe asked, Who do you say I am? Peter responded, saying to xer, You are the salve. Jesus instructed them to tell no one.

But xe began to teach them that the xon of humanity must suffer much and be rejected by the elders and the chief priests and the scribes, and be killed, and rise up on the third day. Xe made this statement matter-of-factly. Peter took xer aside and contested xer, but turning xer back to Peter and facing xer other apprentices, xe said, Get behind me, enemy: you're intent not on what is from the god but what is from humans.

Jesus said, I am the light, illuminating everything. I am everything. Everything comes from me and returns to me. Split a piece of wood, and there I am. Lift up a rock, and you'll find me there. I stood in the middle of the world, in the flesh, for all to see, but I found everyone drunk, no one thirsty. My soul suffered for the xons of humanity because, blind-hearted, they do not see they entered the world empty and will exit empty. They are drunk, but when they sober up they'll be sorry.

And calling to xer the crowd along with xer apprentices xe said to them, Anyone who wants to follow me, let him deny himself and take up his cross and follow me. Whoever wants to preserve his soul will lose it, and whoever loses his soul to me and the good news will preserve it. What does a human profit, who buys the whole world but pays with his soul? And what can a person give to buy back his soul? Whoever is ashamed of me in this faithless, errant generation, of that person will the xon of humanity be ashamed when xe enters into the glory of xer fother and the holy emissaries. The intersection is intimidating, but cross boldly through it. And xe said to them, Truly I tell you that some who stand here will not taste death until they have seen the realm of the god come into power. The emissaries and the prophets give you what you have already. You return it to them, but ought to ask, When will they require of me what is theirs?

Six days later, Jesus took with xer Peter and James and John, and led them up a high hill, off by themselves, and xe changed shape right in front of them, and xer cloak began to shine white as snow, whiter than any cleaner could bleach them. And Elijah with Moses appeared to them, conversing with Jesus. Interpellating himself, Peter said to Jesus, Rabbi, it is beautiful for us to be here; let us make three altars, one for you and one for Moses and one for Elijah. He didn't know what else to say, so afraid they'd grown. And a cloud began to shadow them, and a voice from the cloud declared, This is my xon, my beloved: listen to xer. Xe is life. Xe came from the fother of truth, ineffable and complete, the fother of all that is, the unity of peace, guarantor of the good, timeless life, unblemished joy, perfect harmony of life and faith, timeless life of fotherhood, matherhood, and sisterhood in the rational wisdom that agrees with the mind that in organizing itself organizes all in joyful unity. Xe listens faithfully, respectfully to the one. Xe is the fotherhood, matherhood, sisterhood of rational wisdom, the marriage of truth and rest, the breath of truth in every mind, perfect light of nameless mystery.

Looking around, they saw no one else now, except Jesus alone with them. Jesus operates stealthily, appearing not as xe is, but in a way the viewer can see. Xe appears to the great as great, to the small as small, to the emissaries as an emissary, to humans as a human. In this way xer word hides itself from everyone, so that some who look straight at xer see only themselves. But when xe appeared to xer apprentices on the mountain, xe was great, not small, and xe made the apprentices great so they could see xer in xer greatness.

As they descended the hill xe forcefully charged them to tell no one what they had seen, until the xon of humanity had risen from the dead. They did keep the secret to themselves, though they discussed what rising from the dead might mean. They questioned xer, asking, Why do the scribes say Elijah must come first? Xe answered them, Elijah comes first to restore everything. Is it not written that the xon of humanity must suffer much and be rejected? But I tell you that Elijah has come, and they have done to him what they wanted, exactly as it is written about him.

The apprentices asked Jesus, We know you will leave us; who will be our leader? Jesus said, Wherever you have been, return to James the just, for whose sake sky and earth exist.

The apprentices said to Jesus, Tell us how our end will happen. Jesus replied, Have you understood the beginning so thoroughly that already you ask about the end? At the beginning is the end. Graceful, the one who occupies the beginning: that one will know the end without suffering death.

Xer apprentices asked xer, When will you appear to us? When will we see you? Jesus answered, When you undress without shame, and like little children wad up your clothes at your feet and stamp on them, then you will see the child of the living one and not be afraid.

Xer apprentices asked xer, When will the dead rest? When will the new world arrive? Xe said to them, What you're looking for has happened without your noticing.

When they returned to the other apprentices they saw a large crowd around them and scribes arguing with them. As soon as they saw Jesus, the whole crowd was diverted and ran toward xer to welcome xer. Xe asked them, What are you arguing with them about? One from the crowd said in answer, Teacher, I've brought my son to you: he has an unspeaking breath, and whenever it takes hold of him it throws him down and he foams at the mouth and grinds his teeth and becomes rigid. I asked your apprentices to cast it out, but they couldn't. Xe said in reply, O disbelieving generation, how long will I be with you? How long must I put up with you? Bring him to me. They brought the boy to xer and as soon as it saw xer the breath convulsed the boy and he fell to the ground and spasmed and foamed at the mouth. Jesus asked the father, How long has he had this? He replied, From childhood, and often it has thrown him into fire or into water to destroy him; if possible, have mercy on us and help us. Jesus said to him, If possible? Anything is possible to one who believes.

Immediately the father of the child cried out, I believe; rescue me from my unbelief. Seeing that a crowd was gathering, Jesus threatened the toxic breath, saying to it, Unspeaking and deaf breath, I command you to come out of him and enter him no more. It cried out and badly convulsed the boy and came out of him. He looked so like a corpse that many said he was dead, but Jesus took his hand to help him and he stood up. When Jesus entered the house, xer apprentices in private asked xer, Why were we not able to expel it? Xe told them, The same breath that stokes the fire blows it out. This kind can be forced to depart only by prayer and fasting.

Leaving there, they went along through Galilee, but xe wanted no one to know. In teaching xer apprentices, xe said to them, The xon of humanity will be given over into the hands of men who will kill xer, but three days after xer death xe will stand up. They didn't understand what xe meant, and they were afraid to ask.

When they were back in Capernaum, the collectors of the temple tax approached Peter and asked him, Does your teacher not pay the temple tax? He said, Yes. But when he got to the house, Jesus interrupted, saying, What do you think, Simon? From whom do kings of this world exact taxes, from their own children or from others? He replied, From others. Jesus said to him, Then the children are exempt. Still, just to keep from tripping up others, go to the sea and toss in a hook. In the mouth of the first fish you catch, you'll find a coin: take it to them as the tax for you and me.

They arrived at Capernaum, and in the house xe asked them, What were you discussing along the way? They stayed silent, because along the way they had been discussing which of them would be the greatest. Xe sat down, and calling the twelve together, told them, The one who wants to be first must be last of all, and servant of all. Taking a small child, xe stood it in the center of the group, and embracing the child xe said to them, Whoever receives one such child in my name receives me, and whoever receives me receives not me myself but the one who sent me.

Seeing some infants nursing, Jesus said to xer apprentices, These nursing infants resemble those who enter the realm. They asked xer, so we enter the realm as infants? Xe told them, When you make two one, when you make inside outside and outside inside, and above below, and when you make male and female into one, so that male is not male and female is not female, when you substitute eye for eye, hand for hand, foot for foot, image for image, then you will enter the realm.

John said to him, Teacher, we saw someone expelling visitants in your name, but he was not in our group, so we forbade him. Jesus replied, Don't forbid it; no one who performs a great work in my name will be able soon to speak ill of me. One who is not against us is for us. One who gives you a cup of water to drink because you bear the name of the salve, truly I tell you that one will not be deprived of reward. But whoever trips up one of these trusting little ones, it would be better for that person to have a millstone hung from his neck and be thrown into the sea.

Xe spoke to them, telling them this parable: Who among you, if you had a hundred sheep but lost one, would not leave the ninety-nine at pasture and search for the lost one until you found it? And when you found it, hoist it onto your shoulders, rejoicing? And return home and call together your friends and neighbors, saying, Celebrate with me because I've found the sheep that had been lost. I tell you, in the same way there is in the sky more celebration over one who errs but reconsiders than over ninety-nine so dutiful they never need to reconsider.

And what woman who has ten coins, if she loses one, doesn't light a lamp and sweep her house and search diligently until she finds it? And when she *has* found it, doesn't summon her friends and neighbors, telling them, Celebrate with me; I've found the coin I'd lost? In the same way, I tell you, among the emissaries who stand before the god there is joy when one errant person reconsiders.

Again I say to you, anything on earth that two of you concur about concerning anything you request, it will be done for you by your father in the skies, because wherever two or three commune in my name, there I am with them. Jesus said, If two in one house make peace, they will say to any mountain, Move from there to here, and it will move.

A householder who had everything (children, slaves, cattle, dogs, pigs, wheat, barley, hay, fodder, oil, meat, and acorns) would be savvy enough to know the food proper to each, and would serve children bread and meat, slaves oil and meal, cattle barley, hay, and fodder, dogs bones, and pigs acorns and slop.

Then Peter, approaching xer, said, Boss, how many times must I forgive my brother's errors against me? Seven times? Jesus said to him, I tell you, not seven times, but seventy times seven.

For this reason the realm of the sky resembles a human boss who decided to settle accounts with his slaves. When he started the accounting, one was brought before him who owed ten thousand bucks. Because he could not pay, the boss ordered that he be sold, with his wife and children and everything he had, to make the payment. The slave fell at his feet saying to him, Be patient with me, and I'll pay everything back. The boss of the slave was moved to mercy: he canceled the debt and let him go. But that same slave went off and found a fellow slave who owed him a twenty and he grabbed his throat to choke him, demanding, Pay me what you owe. The fellow slave fell at his feet, saying, Be patient with me, and I'll pay everything back. But he refused him, and went out and had him imprisoned until he could pay the debt. Seeing this, his fellow slaves became very upset, and went to the boss and told him all that had happened. The boss called the slave back to him and said, Worthless slave, I canceled all your debt simply because you asked, but you can't have mercy on your fellow slave the way I had mercy on you?

The boss was angry and gave him to the torturers until he could pay the whole debt. Your fother in the sky will do the same to each of you if you don't from your heart forgive your sibling.

It happened as the day of xer being taken up approached, that xe set xer face intently toward Jerusalem. Xe sent messengers before xer, and they entered a Samaritan village to prepare for xer, but the villagers would not receive xer because xe was intent on continuing to Jerusalem. Seeing this, xer apprentices James and John asked, Boss, do you want us to call down fire from the sky to consume them? But xe turned and chastised them, and then they all went on to another village.

After this, the boss appointed seventy-two others and sent them out two by two, in advance of xer, into all the towns and places xe planned to visit. The seventy-two returned with joy, saying, Boss, even visitants submit to us in your name. Xe said to them, I watched the adversary fall from the sky like lightning. I have kindled a fire in the world, and I am tending it until it blazes. Look, I give you power to step on snakes and scorpions and all the power of the enemy, and nothing will harm you. Still, don't rejoice at the breaths being subject to you; instead, rejoice that your names are written across the skies.

One name cannot be uttered in this world, the name the fother gave the xon. It is the name above all naming, the father's own name. Xon could not become fother without donning the fother's name. Those who belong to this name understand it, but don't speak it; those who don't belong to it don't understand it. Truth generated names in this world for our sake, because we can't pursue truth without names. Truth is one. For our sakes, the many are enabled by love to point toward the one.

And look, a lawyer stood up to test xer, saying, Teacher, what must I do to inherit timeless life? Xe replied to him, What is written in the law? How do you read it? In reply, he said, Love the boss your god with your whole heart and your whole soul and your whole strength and your whole mind, and love your neighbor as much as yourself. Xe said to him, You have answered correctly: do that, and live. But he, wanting to justify himself, said to Jesus, And who is my neighbor? Taking this up, Jesus said, A man going from Jerusalem to Jericho fell among robbers who stripped him of his clothes and beat him and went away, leaving him half dead. By chance a priest was taking the same road, but seeing him he crossed to the other side to pass. Similarly, a Levite at the same place crossed to the other side of the road. But a Samaritan as he traveled reached the same place, and seeing the victim he was moved, and he went to him and bandaged his wounds, treating them with oil and wine, and set him on his own animal and brought him to an inn and took care of him. The next day before he left, he took out two hundred bucks and gave it to the innkeeper and said, Take care of him, and whatever else it costs you I'll repay when I return. Of these three, which one seems to you to have proven a neighbor to the one who fell among thieves? He replied, The one who acted mercifully to him. Jesus said to him, As you go, act in the same way.

During their travels xe entered a certain village, and a woman named Martha received xer. She had a sister named Mary, who sat at Jesus' feet to hear xer word. Martha, frazzled by so much hosting, complained to Jesus, Boss, don't you care that my sister has left me to serve all by myself? But in reply the boss said to her, Martha, Martha, you are taking care and bustling over many things, when only one thing is necessary. Mary has chosen that one urgent thing, and I won't take it from her.

Mary asked, This my body, this my mind: why these tears, why this laughter? The boss answered, The body weeps because it is bound by works; the mind laughs because it is freed from breath. Mary asked xer, Boss, is there a place empty of truth? The boss replied, Anywhere I am not.

Xe said to them, Who among you does not have a friend you could go to at midnight to request, Friend, lend me three loaves; a friend traveling along the road has stopped in, and I have nothing to offer him? What such friend will answer by saying, Don't disturb me; my door is shut, and I and my children are in bed, I can't get up now and give you anything? I tell you, even if he won't rise and offer the bread for friendship's sake, merely to rid himself of annoyance he'll rise and give all you need.

It happened, as xe was saying these things, that a woman in the crowd spoke up and declared to xer, Graceful the womb that gave you birth, and the breasts you sucked! But xe replied, Graceful, instead, those who hear the word of the god and obey it.

Turning to the leaders of the people, xe spoke this word: Read the writings. Recognize that in them you have life. They are the witnesses regarding me. Don't think I came to accuse you to my fother. Your accuser is Moses, in whom you had hoped. They replied, We know the god spoke to Moses, but we don't know where your words come from. Jesus answered them, Now what accuses you is your disbelief of Moses' testimony. If you believed Moses, you'd believe me.

After xe had spoken, a Pharisee invited xer to dinner, so xe entered and reclined. The Pharisee, seeing this, wondered to himself why Jesus had not washed before dinner. The boss said to him, You Pharisees clean the outside of the cup and the plate, but inside you yourselves are full of greed and malice. You mindless people, didn't the one who made the outside make the inside, too? Give what you have to those in need; then, look, everything is clean for you. But oh you, you Pharisees, you tithe mint and rue and other herbs, but skip over justice and love of the god. Those you should practice, without leaving the other undone. Oh you, you Pharisees, you love the prime seats in the synagogues and greetings in the town square. Oh you, you are like unmarked graves that people walk over without knowing it.

One of the lawyers fired back, saying to xer, Teacher, in saying this you also insult us. But Jesus said, Oh you, you lawyers, too. You load others with burdensome loads that you yourselves don't touch with even one of your fingers. A curse on you, who rebuild the tombs of the prophets your fathers killed, affirming your fathers' murders, their killing the ones whose tombs you rebuild. This is why the wisdom of the god says, I send them prophets and envoys, some of whom they kill and persecute, so that all the blood shed by prophets from the foundation of the world will be charged to this generation, from the blood of Abel to the blood of Zechariah, who was killed between the altar and the temple. I tell you, it will be charged against this generation. Oh you, you lawyers, you have taken away the key of knowledge. You yourselves haven't entered in, only prevented the entry of others.

Xe delivered a parable to the invited guests, having noticed that they were selecting the places of honor, saying to them, When you are invited by anyone to a wedding, don't recline at the first seat, in case a more distinguished guest than you has been invited, and the one who invited you both come and say to you, Give this place to the guest, and you be forced to take the lowest seat, in humiliation. Instead, when you are invited, go and recline in the last seat, so the host, seeing you there, may say to you, Friend, move farther up. Then you will be respected by the others at the table. Whoever promotes himself will be humbled, and whoever humbles himself will be promoted.

Then xe said to one who had invited xer, when you host a lunch or dinner, don't invite your friends or siblings or kin or your wealthy neighbors, in case they return the favor, paying you back. Instead, when you host a meal, invite persons who are poor or infirm or unable to walk or unable to see; then you will be graceful, not recompensed by them but rewarded at the standing up of the just.

Another of the guests, hearing this, said to xer, Graceful the one who eats bread in the realm of the god. Jesus said to him, A man giving a large banquet invited many guests, and at the hour sent his slave to tell those who were invited, Come; everything is ready now. But they all began to make excuses. The first said to him, I have bought a plot of ground and must go see it; please excuse me. Another said, I've bought five yoke of oxen, and I'm on my way to try them out; please excuse me. Another said, I have married a wife, and because of this I can't come. So the slave returned and reported these regrets to his boss. In his anger, the master of the house said to his slave, Go quickly into the streets and alleys of the city and bring back with you persons who are poor or infirm or unable to walk or unable to see. And the slave said, Boss, I've done what you said to, and still there's room. So the boss said to the slave, Go farther, out to the roads and highways, and urge more to come, until the house is full. Truly I tell you, none of those who were invited first will taste this meal.

Xe said, A man had two sons, and the younger of them said to his father, Father, give me the part of the estate that falls to me. So he divided his living between them. Not many days later, the younger son packed everything and journeyed to a distant country and there wasted his substance by living recklessly. When he had spent all he had, there occurred in that land a famine, and he sank into need. So he went and attached himself to a citizen of that country, who sent him to his fields to feed the pigs. He hungered even for the husks the pigs ate; no one gave him anything. When he came to himself, he said, How many of my father's hired hands have plenty of bread, and I'm wasting away in hunger. I'll rise up and go to my father and say to him, Father, I have erred under the sky and in your sight; I'm not worthy to be called your son. Make me like one of your hired hands. And he rose up and went to his father. While he was still a long way off, his father saw him and was moved, and ran and threw his arms around his neck and kissed him. The son said to him, Father, I have erred under the sky and in your sight; I'm not worthy to be called your son. But the father said to his slaves, Quick, bring the best robe and put it on him, and put a ring on his hand and shoes on his feet, and bring the fattened calf and kill it, and let's eat and celebrate, because this my son was dead and now he's alive, he was lost but he's found. So they ate and celebrated.

The older son had been out in the field. Returning, as he neared the house he heard music and dancing, and he called to one of the slave boys and asked what this meant. He told him, Your brother has come, and your father has killed the fattened calf, because he has returned safely. He was angry, and wouldn't enter. His father came out and pleaded with him, but answering his father he said, Look, all these years I've slaved for you and never disobeyed your command, but you never gave me even a young goat so I could feast with my friends. But your son who has devoured your living with whores returns, and for him you kill the fattened calf. And he replied, Son, you are with me always, and all that is mine is yours. But it's right to celebrate and rejoice, because your brother was dead and now he's alive, he was lost but he's found.

By the time xe left there, the scribes and Pharisees had filled themselves with anger, and determined to egg xer on, to get xer to say something they could use against xer.

⸸

After these things Jesus walked around through Galilee, but chose not to walk around in Judea because the Jews sought to kill xer. The Jewish festival of tabernacles was soon, so xer siblings said to xer, Leave here and go to Judea, so that the apprentices will see the works you perform: no one performs in secret who seeks to be famous. If you do these things, show yourself to the world. Even xer siblings did not believe in xer. Jesus told them, My time isn't here yet; your time is always here. The world can't hate you, but it hates me because I testify against it, that its works are harmful. You go to the festival; I'm not going to the festival, because my time hasn't yet fully arrived. Having said this, xe remained in Galilee.

But after xer siblings had gone to the festival, xe too went, not openly but in secret. The Jews searched for xer at the festival, asking Where is xe? There was a lot of grumbling about xer in the crowds: some said, Xe's good, but others said, No, xe leads the crowd astray. But no one spoke openly about xer, from fear of the Jews.

But about the middle of the festival Jesus went up to the temple and taught. The Jews were amazed, asking, How can xe be literate, but have no learning? Jesus answered them, and said, My teaching is not mine, but xers who sent me. One who wills to do xer will will know of this teaching whether it is from the god or whether I assert it on my own. One who talks about himself seeks his own glory; the one who seeks the glory of xer who sent xer is true, and no injustice is in xer. Didn't Moses give you the law? But none of you fulfill the law. Why do you seek to kill me? The crowd responded, You have a visitant; who seeks to kill you? Jesus answered, and said to them, I did one work, and you're all amazed. Moses gave you circumcision — not that it's from Moses himself, but from the fathers — and you'll circumcise a man on the sabbath. You can circumcise a man on the sabbath without breaking the law of Moses, but you're angry with me when I make a man whole on the sabbath? Don't judge by appearance, but judge with just judgment.

Some of the people from Jerusalem said, Isn't this the one they're seeking to kill? But look, xe speaks openly and they say nothing. Maybe the principals really know that this is the salve? But we know where xe's from; when the salve comes, no one will know where xe's from. So Jesus spoke out as xe taught in the temple, and said, You know me and you know where I'm from. I didn't come here on my own, but the one who sent me is true, the one you don't know. I know xer, because I am of xer, and xe sent me. Who hears me hears who sent me. They were intent on arresting xer, but no one laid a hand on xer, because xer hour had not come yet. And many from the crowd believed in xer and said, When the salve comes, will xe perform more signs than this one has?

The Pharisees heard the crowd mutterings some things about xer, and the chief priests and Pharisees sent officers to arrest xer. Jesus told them, I'm with you a little while longer, and then I go to the one who sent me. You'll seek me but you won't find me: I'll be where you can't go. The Jews asked one another, Where will xe go that we won't find xer? Will xe go to those scattered among the Greeks, and teach the Greeks? What's the sense of her saying, You'll seek me but you won't find me: I'll be where you can't go?

On the last day, the great day, of the festival, Jesus stood and cried out, saying, If you're thirsty, come to me and drink. The one who believes on me, as the writing says, from the belly of that person will flow rivers of living water. Xe said this about the breath that those who believed on xer would receive, but there was no such breath yet, because Jesus was not yet glorified.

Hearing these words, some from the crowd said, Truly this is the prophet. Others said, This is the salve. Some said, Surely the salve can't come from Galilee? Doesn't the writing say the salve will come from David's descendants and from Bethlehem, the village David was from? Division occurred in the crowd because of xer. Some wanted to arrest xer, but no one laid a hand on xer.

Then the officers returned to the chief priests and Pharisees, who asked them, Why didn't you bring xer? The officers answered,

No man ever spoke like this. The Pharisees replied to them, Surely you haven't been duped, too? Surely no one from the principals or the Pharisees believes in xer? But this crowd, not knowing the law, is cursed. Nicodemus, the one who earlier came to xer, and who was one of them, said, Surely our law doesn't judge anyone without first hearing the person and knowing what the person has done? In answer they said to him, Aren't you from Galilee, too? Look, and you'll see that no prophets arise from Galilee.

╬

Someone from the crowd said, Teacher, tell my brother to divide the inheritance with me. Jesus replied to him, Man, who appointed me judge over your case? Addressing the crowd, xe said, Take care to guard against always wanting more: a person's life is not increased by increased possessions. Giving them a parable, xe said, The land of a rich man yielded bountifully. He thought to himself, What should I do? I don't have enough storage for all this grain. He said, I'll do this: I'll tear down my barns and build bigger ones, and store my grain in them. I'll say to my soul, Soul, you have built up enough reserve for many years, so take it easy now: eat, drink, and be merry. But the god said to him, Senseless one, this very night your life is demanded of you; now who will own all this you've accumulated? So it goes for one who preserves for himself but is not rich toward the god.

Stay suited up, with your lamp lit. Be like slaves waiting for their boss to return from a wedding feast, so that when he arrives and knocks they can open up immediately. Graceful, such slaves, who when the boss returns stand ready: truly I tell you, he will put on an apron himself, and reward them with a meal he himself serves them. If he arrives late at night or even into the morning and finds them still ready, graceful are such slaves. Keep this in mind, too, that a homeowner who knew when the thief was coming wouldn't let the thief into the house. You, too, must be prepared, because the xon of humanity will arrive when you are not expecting xer.

Then Peter asked xer, Boss, are you addressing this parable to us, or to everyone? The boss replied, Who is that faithful, prudent manager that the boss stations above the others, to distribute their allowance to them on time? Graceful, such a slave, found doing his work when the boss shows up. In truth I say to you, he will put that one in charge of everything he has. But if that same slave says in his heart, The boss will be late coming back, and begins to beat the slave boys and slave girls, and eat and drink until he's drunk, the boss will arrive on a day the slave does not expect, at an hour when he isn't alert, and the boss will cut him off and return him back among the untrustworthy. That slave, who knew what the boss assigned him but did not fulfill it, will be whipped with many lashes. To whom much is given, from that person much is required; to whom much is assigned, from that person much will be demanded.

Xer apprentices challenged xer, Who are you to say such things to us? Xe replied, You haven't put together who I am from what I say. You're like ones who love the tree but hate its fruit, or love the fruit but hate the tree. You see me in yourself as you see yourself in water or a mirror.

Just then some people arrived telling Jesus news of some Galileans whose blood Pilate had mingled with the blood of their sacrifices. In response, xe said, Do you think, because they suffered in this way, these Galileans had erred more than other Galileans? No, I tell you, but unless you reconsider, you all will also be lost. Or those eighteen killed when a tower collapsed on them in Siloam: do you think they were more errant than anyone else in Jerusalem? No, I tell you, but unless you reconsider, you all also will be lost.

Then xe told them this parable: A person had a fig tree planted in his garden, but when he looked for fruit from it he found none, so he said to the gardener, Look, for three years now I've been coming to this tree looking for fruit but finding none. Cut it down. Why let it deplete the soil? But in reply the gardener said, Boss, leave it just one more year and let me dig in manure around it. If it bears fruit after that, great, and if not, *then* cut it down.

The days will come when vines will grow, each with ten thousand branches, and on each branch ten thousand twigs, on each twig ten thousand shoots, on each shoot ten thousand clusters, on each cluster ten thousand grapes, and from each pressed grape will flow twenty-five gallons of wine. And any time a holy one picks a cluster, another will cry out, I'm a better cluster, pick me, bless the boss through me! Similarly, each stalk of wheat will grow ten thousand heads, each head ten thousand grains, and from each grain will come ten pounds of finest flour. In the same way, other fruits and grains and vegetables will produce past all proportion. And all the animals that feed themselves from this bounty of the earth will live in peace and harmony with one another, and in complete subjection to humanity.

Even forces for harm advance the good, since the holy breath leads them to believe they get for themselves what they give the good. Because of this, when an apprentice one day asked the boss for something from this world, xe said, Ask your mather; she will give you something from another.

Xe was teaching in one of the synagogues on the sabbath, and, look, there was a woman who for eighteen years had had a debilitating breath that bent her far forward and wouldn't let her straighten up. When Jesus saw her, xe called her over and said to her, Woman, you are released from your debility. Xe put xer hands on her, and immediately she straightened up and praised the god. But the head of the synagogue, indignant because Jesus had healed on the sabbath, said to the crowd, There are six days on which to work: come for healing on one of those days, not on the sabbath. But the boss responded, saying, Hypocrites, doesn't each of you on the sabbath release your ox or donkey from the stall and lead it to water? Shouldn't this woman, a daughter of Abraham, bound by the adversary for eighteen years, be released from this bond on the sabbath day? When xe had said this, xer opponents were put to shame, and the crowd celebrated the marvelous deeds xe was doing.

King Herod heard, because Jesus' name had spread around, with people saying, John the baptizer has been raised from the dead, and that's why these powers are at work in xer. Others said, Xe is Elijah. Others said xe was a prophet like the old prophets. But when Herod heard of xer, he said, John, though I beheaded him, has risen.

At that very hour, some Pharisees came to xer and said, Go away from here, because Herod wants to kill you. Xe said to them,

Go tell that fox, I expel visitants and perform healings today and tomorrow, and on the next day I accomplish my purpose. So I must continue on my course today and tomorrow and the next day, because it wouldn't do for a prophet to die outside Jerusalem.

Jerusalem, Jerusalem, xe cried, that kills the prophets and stones the envoys sent you. How often have I wanted to gather your children the way a hen gathers her brood under her wing, but you were unwilling. Look, your house is abandoned. I tell you, you will not see me again until you say, Blessings on the one who comes in the name of the boss.

Xe said to xer apprentices, A rich man had someone to manage his holdings. When he began to be told that the manager was wasting his goods, he called the manager to him and said, What's this I hear about you? Give an account of your management, or you're no longer the manager. The manager thought to himself, What will I do if the boss takes back the management from me? I'm not strong enough to dig; I'm ashamed to beg. I know what I'll do so that when I'm fired from management, people still will welcome me into their homes. So, calling in his boss's debtors one by one, he asked the first, How much do you owe the boss? That person replied, A hundred jugs of oil. The manager told him, Take your note and quickly sit down and write out one for fifty. He asked another, How much do you owe? That person replied, A hundred bushels of wheat. The manager told him, Take your note and write out one for eighty. The boss commended the dishonest manager for his shrewdness, because the children of the time are more shrewd in dealing with the shrewd than the children of the light are. So I tell you, Use your dirty money to win friends, so that after it's gone you'll still have a place to go. One who is faithful in trivial matters is faithful in important matters, and one who is unfaithful in trivial matters is unfaithful in important matters. If you haven't been faithful with your dirty money, who will entrust to you true wealth? And if you haven't been faithful with what belongs to someone else, who will give you anything for your own?

The money-loving Pharisees heard all this and scoffed at xer. But xe told them, You're the type to justify yourselves in the sight of people, but the god knows your hearts, and what humans prize, the god detests. It satisfies you to see your likeness, but it will weigh you down when you discern the images that precede you, that never die but never show themselves.

There was a rich man, dressed in purple and fine linen, who ate sumptuously every day, and at his gate lay a beggar named Lazarus, covered with sores, who wanted the crumbs that fell from the rich man's table. The dogs licked at his sores. It happened that the beggar died and was carried by emissaries to Abraham's embrace. The rich man, too, died and was buried. In Hades, in torment, he looked up and saw, far away, Abraham with Lazarus in his embrace. Crying out, he said, Father Abraham, have pity on me, and send Lazarus to dip the tip of his finger in water and cool my tongue: I'm in torment in this fire. Abraham replied, Child, remember that in your lifetime you received your good things, and Lazarus by contrast received bad. Now he is comforted and you are tormented. Besides all that, between us and you a vast chasm yawns, so that no one who *would* pass across from here to you *could*, and no one can pass from there to us. He said, Then I beg you, father, send him to my father's house, where I have five brothers; let him warn them, so that they don't also come to this place of torment. Abraham said to him, They have Moses and the prophets; let them listen to them. And he said, No, father Abraham, but if someone from the dead went to them, they would reconsider. But he replied to him, If they won't listen to Moses and the prophets, they won't be persuaded even by someone risen from the dead.

The envoys said to the boss, Secure our faith. The boss replied, If you had faith even the size of a mustard seed, you could say to this mulberry tree, Uproot yourself from here and plant yourself in the sea, and it would obey you.

Which of you would say to your slave, just in from plowing or from tending sheep, Have a seat for dinner? Wouldn't you tell the slave instead, Make my dinner, clean up, and wait on me while I eat and drink, before you yourself eat and drink? Would you thank the slave for doing what he was commanded to do? So should it be with you. When you have done all you've been commanded to do, say, We are unexceptional slaves, having done only what it was our duty to do.

Humanity should imitate the wise fisher who, casting the net and then drawing it up full of many small fish, found one large fish and kept it, returning the others to the sea. Anyone with ears to hear, hear. The dreamer will rule, and the ruler will sleep. What one ear hears from the other ear, proclaim from the housetops. Be passersby.

It happened as xe was going to Jerusalem that xe passed the region between Samaria and Galilee. Entering one village, xe encountered ten persons with leprosy, who stood at a distance. Raising their voices, they called to xer, Jesus, overseer, have mercy on us. Seeing them, xe said to them, Go and present yourselves to the priests. It happened even as they were on their way that they were made clean. One of them, seeing that she was healed, returned, in a loud voice praising the god. And she fell at Jesus' feet, thanking xer. She was a Samaritan. In response to her, Jesus said, Weren't ten made clean? Where are the other nine? Did none find it in themselves to return to praise the god except this alien? And xe said to her, Rise and go. Your faith has healed you.

Asked by Pharisees when the realm of the god would occur, xe replied, the realm of the god is not something to be observed. No one will say, Look, here it is, or Look, there it is. Instead, the realm of the god is within you. Unless you make the right like the left and the left like the right and the up like the down and the before like the after, you will not recognize the realm. The god is a dyer. As good dyes, true dyes, saturate the things dyed with them, so things dyed with the god's immortal dyes become immortal.

Xe said to xer apprentices, The day is coming when you will long to see even one of the days of the xon of humanity, but you won't see it. They'll say to you, Look, xe's there, or Look, xe's here, but don't follow after them. As lightning flashes, lighting the sky from one horizon to the other, so in xer own day will the xon of humanity be, but first xe must suffer many things and be rejected by this generation. As it was in the days of Noah, so will it be in the days of the xon of humanity. They ate, drank, married, gave in marriage, right up to the day Noah boarded the ark and the flood came and destroyed them all. Similarly, as it was in the days of Lot: they ate, drank, bought, sold, planted, built, but the day Lot left

Sodom, fire rained down from the sky and the god destroyed them all. That's how it will be on the day the xon of humanity is revealed. On that day, the one who is on a housetop had best not return indoors to retrieve valuables, and the one who is in the field had best not return home. Remember Lot's wife. Whoever tries to preserve his life will lose it, but the one who loses his life will preserve it. I tell you, in that night there will be two men in one bed: one will be taken and the other left. Two women will be grinding meal: one will be taken and the other left. And they questioned xer, asking, Where, boss? Xe told them, Where the corpse is, vultures gather. Before the salve some came from a realm they could not reenter, and went to one they could not leave. Then the salve arrived. Those who had gone in xe let out, and those who had gone out xe let in.

In a certain city there was a judge who neither feared the god nor respected humanity, and in that same city lived a widow who kept coming to him, demanding, Give me justice against my opponent. For a time he refused, but eventually he said to himself, Though I neither fear the god nor respect humanity, still this widow so pesters me that I'll give her justice just to end the annoyance. And the boss said, Listen to what this unjust judge says. Will not the god give justice to xer elect who cry to him night and day, not put them off? I tell you, xe will give them justice swiftly. But when the xon of humanity comes, will xe find such faith anywhere on earth?

To some who were smug about their own justice and dismissive of others, xe told this parable. Two men entered the temple to pray, one of them a Pharisee and the other a broker. The Pharisee stood prominently and prayed about himself, Thank you, god, that I am not like other people: robbers, cheaters, adulterers, or this broker. I fast twice a week, and tithe from all my income. The broker stood to the side, and wouldn't look toward the sky. He beat his breast and prayed, God, be merciful toward my errancy. I tell you, this one, not the other, returned home justified. All who promote themselves will be humbled, and all who humble themselves will be promoted.

Xe arose and went from there to the region of Judea, beyond the Jordan, and the crowds kept gathering around xer, and as was xer way, xe taught them. The Pharisees approached xer, and as a test put to xer the question whether it's permissible for a man to divorce his wife. In reply, xe asked them, What did Moses command you? They said, It's permitted by Moses to write a declaration of dismissal, and divorce her. Jesus said to them, Because of your hardheartedness he wrote in this loophole for you. But from the beginning of creation *they were made male and female, and a man should leave behind his mother and father and hold tightly to his wife, and the two of them be one flesh.* So they are not two, but one flesh. What the god has united, let no human divide. In the house, xer apprentices asked the same question, and xe told them, Whoever divorces one wife to marry another commits adultery, and whoever divorces one husband to marry another commits adultery.

Xer apprentices complained, If that's how things stand for a man and woman, it's not smart to marry. Xe replied, This principle applies not to everyone, only to those to whom it was given. Some were born genderqueer, some became genderqueer in their environment, and some have made themselves genderqueer for the sake of the realm of the skies. Anyone able to embrace this, embrace it.

The apprentices scolded some people who had brought young children to xer, to have xer touch them. Seeing this, Jesus was displeased, and told them, Let the children come to me, don't prevent them, because the realm of the god belongs to just such. Truly I tell you, whoever does not receive the realm of the god like a child will not enter into it. Embracing the children and putting xer hands on them, xe blessed them.

As xe was heading out on the road, a man ran up and knelt before xer and asked xer, Good teacher, what must I do to inherit timeless life? Jesus asked him, Why do you call me good? No one is good but the one god. You know the commandments, *don't murder, don't commit adultery, don't steal, don't bear false witness, don't defraud, honor your father and mother.* He replied, Teacher, from youth I have observed all these. Jesus, looking at him, loved him, and said to him, You lack one thing: go, sell everything you own and give to the poor, and you will have treasure in the sky. And follow me. He was disappointed by xer reply, and went away miserable, because he had many possessions.

Jesus turned around, and said to xer apprentices, How difficult it is for those who have wealth to enter the realm of the god. The apprentices wondered at these words. Jesus, answering again, said to them, Children, how difficult it is to enter the realm of the god. It's easier for a camel to pass through the eye of a needle than for a rich person to enter the realm of the god. They were even more amazed, murmuring among themselves, Then who can be preserved? Looking at them, Jesus said, For humans impossible, but not for the god. For the god, everything is possible. Then Peter began to speak to xer, Look, we've left everything and followed you. Jesus answered, Truly I tell you, no one who has left home and brothers and sisters and mother and father and children and lands for my sake and for the sake of the good news will not receive now for this moment a hundred times those homes and brothers and sisters and mothers and fathers in persecutions, but in the age to come timeless life. Many who are first will be last, many last, first.

The realm of the skies resembles a human householder who went out at dawn to hire workers for her vineyard. Coming to terms with the workers for ten bucks a day, she sent them out into the vineyard. Going out around nine, she saw others standing idle in the town square, and she said to them, You, too, go to the vineyard, and whatever is just I'll pay you. Around noon and then at three she went again, and did the same thing each time. Around five she went again and found still others standing around, and asked them, Why stand here idle all day? They said to her, Because no one hired us. She said to them, You, too, go to the vineyard. When evening came, the boss of the vineyard said to her foreman, Call the workers and pay them their wages, starting with the last and ending with the first. Those who'd been hired at five came and received ten bucks each. When the ones hired first came, they thought they'd get more, but each got ten bucks. When they received it, they groused to the householder, saying, These who got here last only worked an hour, but you've made them equal to us who bore the burden and the heat of the whole day. But in reply she said to one of them, Friend, I've done you no injustice. Didn't you agree with me to ten bucks? Take what's yours, and go. I choose to give this latest-hired what I give you. Am I not allowed to do what I want with what is mine? Is your eye envious because I'm being generous? So is it that the last are first and the first last.

They were on the road going up to Jerusalem, with Jesus leading the way, and xer followers were perplexed and fearful. Xe took aside the twelve again, and began to tell them what was about to happen to xer: Look, we're going up to Jerusalem, and the xon of humanity will be given over to the chief priests and the scribes, who will condemn xer to death and pass xer on to the others, who will mock xer and whip xer and spit on xer and kill xer, but after three days xe will stand up.

Xer apprentices said to xer, Twenty-four prophets have spoken in Israel, and they all spoke of you. Xe replied, When you defer to the dead, you disregard the one living among you.

Jesus said to xer apprentices, Compare me to something, to say what I am like. Simon Peter said to xer, You are like a just emissary. Matthew said to xer, You are like a wise philosopher. Thomas said to xer, Teacher, my mouth cannot say what you are like. Jesus replied, I am not your teacher once you have drunk your fill from the spring I tend. Xe took Thomas aside and spoke three sayings to him. When Thomas returned to his companions they asked him, What did Jesus say to you? Thomas replied, If I told you even one thing xe said, you would pick up rocks to stone me, and fire would leap from the rocks and consume you.

Approaching xer, James and John, the sons of Zebedee, said to xer, Teacher, we want you to do for us whatever we ask. Xe replied, What do you want me to do for you? They said to xer, Grant us to sit one on your right and one on your left, in your glory. But Jesus said to them, You don't know what you're asking. Are you able to drink the cup I drink or be baptized with the baptism I am baptized with? They said to xer, We're able. Jesus said to them, You will drink the cup I drink and be baptized with the baptism I am baptized with, but to sit on my right and on my left is not mine to give: those seats will go to those for whom they've been designated. Hearing this, the other ten began to be indignant with James and

John. But calling them to xer, Jesus told them, You know that for the others those recognized as rulers do rule over them, and those who are empowered exert their power. But not so among you. Whoever wants to be great among you must be your servant, and whoever wants first place among you must be the slave of all, because the xon of humanity came not to be served but to serve, and to give xer soul in ransom for many.

They went to Jericho, and as xe and xer apprentices and a big crowd were leaving Jericho, Bartimaeus the son of Timaeus, a blind beggar, sat on the roadside. Hearing that it was Jesus of Nazareth, he began to call out, saying, Xon of David, have mercy on me. Many told him to shut up, but he shouted louder, Xon of David, have mercy on me. Jesus stopped and said, Call him here. So they called the blind man, saying to him, Take heart, get up, xe's calling you. Tossing off his cloak, he jumped up and went to Jesus. Responding to him, Jesus said, What do you want me to do for you? The blind man said to xer, Rabbi, I want to see. And Jesus said to him, Go; your faith has healed you. Immediately he could see, and followed xer along the road.

Jesus performed in the presence of xer apprentices many other signs not written in this book. These are written so you may believe that Jesus is the salve the xon of the god, and by believing have life in xer name.

Xe entered Jericho, and was passing through town. A man named Zacchaeus was a broker, and very wealthy. He tried to see Jesus, but couldn't see over the crowd, because he was small in stature, so he ran ahead and climbed up a sycamore tree, to watch from it when Jesus passed by. When Jesus got there, xe noticed him, and said, Zacchaeus, hurry and come down, so I can stop at your house today. So he quickly came down, and welcomed xer gladly. Seeing this, the people all grumbled to one another, Xe's gone to stay with a corrupt man. Zacchaeus stood up and said to the boss, So, boss, today I give half my possessions to the poor, and if I've extorted anything from anyone I will give back four times as much. And Jesus said to them, Today salvation has happened in this house, and now he too is a son of Abraham. The xon of humanity has come to seek and to preserve the lost.

╬

When they were nearing Jerusalem, at Bethpage and Bethany near the Mount of Olives, xe sent two of xer apprentices ahead, saying to them, Go into the village ahead of you, and as soon as you enter it you'll find tied there a colt that has not yet been ridden. Untie it and lead it here. If anyone asks you, Why are you doing this?, say, The boss has need of it, and will return it soon. So they went, and found a colt tied at the entrance to a winding street, and they untied it. Some who were standing there asked them, What are you doing, untying this colt? They said what Jesus told them to say, so the ones there let them do it. And they led the colt to Jesus, and spread their cloaks on it, and xe sat on it. And many spread out their cloaks on the road, and others strewed leafy stalks they'd cut from the fields. Those who preceded and those who followed shouted out,

     Help.

         Blessed be the one who comes in the name of the boss,
         blessed be the coming of the realm of our father David.
     Help from the highest.

Some of the Pharisees in the crowd said to xer, Teacher, tell your apprentices to shut up. But xe replied to them, I tell you, if these kept silent, the stones would cry out.

As xe approached the city, seeing it xe wept over it, saying, If only you recognized, even for this one day, what brings peace, but now it is hidden from your eyes. The day will come when your enemies will surround you and lay siege and attack you from every side, and level you, and your children with you, leaving not one stone atop another stone, because you didn't recognize in time that you'd been visited.

When fire has consumed everything, when it can find nothing else to burn, it extinguishes itself.

Xe entered into Jerusalem and went into the temple, but looking around at everything, seeing that it was evening, xe went out to Bethany with the twelve.

The next day, leaving Bethany, xe was hungry, and seeing in the distance a fig tree in leaf, xe went to look for fruit on it, but when xe reached it xe found no fruit, because it wasn't the season for figs. Responding to this, xe said to the tree, From now on, no one will eat fruit from you, ever. The apprentices heard xer.

They arrived at Jerusalem, and xe entered the temple and began to drive out those who sold and bought in the temple, and xe over-turned the moneychangers' tables and the seats of the dovesellers, and permitted no one to carry a jar through the temple. Xe told the dovesellers, Take these away. Don't make my fother's house a house of commerce. And xe taught, saying, Is it not written that

My house will be called a house of prayer for all ethnicities? But you have made it a hideout for robbers. Xer disciples remembered that it was written,

Zeal for your house will consume me.

Taking them with xer, xe led them into the sanctuary itself, walking straight through the temple. One Pharisee, a high priest named Levi, confronted them, saying to the preserver, Who gave you permission to tramp into this sanctuary and see the sacred vessels, when you haven't bathed and your apprentices haven't washed their feet? You're dirty, but you tramp through this tem-ple, a clean place no one else unbathed and badly dressed tramps through, looking on the sacred vessels. The preserver, standing by xer apprentices, answered him, You who stay here in the temple, are you yourself so clean? The Pharisee insisted, Yes, I'm clean: I bathed in the pool of David, entering the water by one set of steps and leaving by another, then putting on clothes that are white and clean, only then coming here and gazing on the sacred vessels. In answer to him the preserver said, Too bad you're blind to what you should see. You've washed with water in which, day and night, dogs and pigs have splashed. In your bath you washed your outside, your skin, the same outside that prostitutes and dancing girls wash and oil and preen to prick the lusts of men, while inside they're full of scorpions and all sorts of ills. My apprentices and I, though you accuse us of uncleanliness, have been washed by waters of lasting life.

In reply, the Jews asked xer, What sign do you show us, to validate your doing this? In answer, Jesus said to them, Raze this temple and in three days I will raise it. The Jews said, It's taken forty-six years to build this temple, and you'll raise it in three days? But xe spoke of the temple of xer body. After xe rose from death, the apprentices remembered xer saying this, and they believed the writings and the word Jesus had spoken. The chief priests and scribes heard this, and sought some way to destroy xer. They feared xer, because the whole crowd was struck by xer teaching. When evening came, Jesus and the twelve left the city.

As they went along in the morning, they saw the fig tree withered to its roots. Peter remembered it, and said to xer, Rabbi, look, the fig tree you cursed has withered. In reply, Jesus said to them, Have faith in god. Truly I tell you, whoever says to this hill, Be picked up and tossed into the sea, and does not doubt in his heart, but believes that what he says will happen, it will be done for him. Because of this I tell you, everything you ask for in prayer, believe you have received it and it is yours, and when you stand praying, if you hold anything against anyone, let it go, so that your fother in the skies will release you from your failings.

They went again into Jerusalem, and as xe was walking in the temple, the chief priests and scribes and elders came to xer and challenged xer, By what authority do you do these things? And who gave you the authority to do such things? Jesus said to them, I'll ask you a question. Answer it, and I'll tell you by what authority I do these things. Was the baptism of John from the sky or from humans? Answer me that. They thought it through among them-selves, figuring, If we say, From the sky, xe'll say, Then why didn't you believe him?, but we can't say, From humans. They feared the crowd, because everyone took John to be a real prophet. So in re-ply to Jesus they said, We can't tell. So Jesus said, Then I won't tell you by what authority I do these things.

How does it seem to you? A man had two children, and going to the first, he said, Kid, go work today in the vineyard. In reply the child said, I don't want to, but later reconsidered and went. Going to the other child the father said the same thing, and in reply the child said, I'm going, boss, but didn't go. Of the two, which did the will of the father? They said, The first. Jesus said to them, Truly I tell you, crooks and whores will enter the realm of the god before you, because John came to you in the way of justice, and you didn't believe him, but the crooks and whores believed him, and even when you saw that, you still didn't change your minds and believe him.

Listen to another parable. A householder planted a vineyard, put a fence around it, dug a winepress in it, and built a watchtower. Then he leased it to tenants and traveled to another country. As harvest season neared, he sent his slaves to the tenants to collect his share. But the tenants seized his slaves and beat one, killed another, and stoned the third, so he sent other slaves, more than the first time, but the tenants did the same to them. Finally he sent his own son to them, saying, They will respect my son. But the tenants, seeing the son, said to one another, This is his heir. Let's kill him and scam his inheritance. So they grabbed him, dragged him out of the vineyard, and killed him. When the boss of the vineyard himself comes, what will he do to the tenants? They said to xer, He will murder the murderers, and lease the vineyard to other tenants, who will give him his share when it's due. Jesus said to them, I tell you, for this reason the realm of the god will be taken from you and given to others who will tend its harvest. Have you never read this in the writings,

> The stone the builders rejected
> has become the cornerstone;
> the boss has done this,
> and it is marvelous to our eyes?

Whoever falls on this stone will be shattered; whoever it falls on will be crushed.

Hearing xer parables, the chief priests and Pharisees recognized that xe spoke about them. They wanted to arrest xer, but they feared the crowd, who thought xer a prophet.

They sent some Pharisees and Herodians to catch xer in xer words. They went, and said to xer, Teacher, we know you are truthful, favoring no one because you don't look to human reputation but instead teach the way of the god according to the truth. Is it right to pay taxes to Caesar or not? Should we pay them or not pay them?

Seeing their hypocrisy, xe said to them, Why do you test me? Bring me a coin to look at. They brought one, and xe said to them, Whose image is this, and whose inscription? They answered xer, Caesar's. Jesus said to them, Give back to Caesar what is of Caesar, and to the god what is of the god. They were amazed by xer.

That same day, some Sadducees approached xer. They say there is no standing up, so they asked xer, Teacher, Moses said, If someone who has no children dies, his brother should marry his widow and have offspring for him. Suppose there were seven brothers. The first married and died without descendants, so the wife passed to his brother. The same happened with this second brother, and the third, and so on through the seventh. Finally the woman herself died. In the standing up, of the seven whose wife will she be, since they all married her? In reply, Jesus said to them, You've gone astray, not knowing the writings or the power of the god. In the standing up, they don't marry or give in marriage, but are like emissaries in the sky. As for the standing up of the dead, have you not read what was said to you by the god, I am the god of Abraham and the god of Isaac and the god of Jacob? Xe is not the god of the dead but of the living. Hearing this, the crowds were astonished by xer teaching.

The Pharisees, hearing xe'd silenced the Sadducees, gathered around xer, and one of them, a lawyer, posed xer a question, Teacher, what is the greatest commandment in the law? Xe said to him, Love your boss the god with your whole heart and your whole soul and your whole mind. That is the greatest commandment, and the first. The second is similar, Love your neighbor like yourself. From these two commandments hang the whole law and the prophets.

While the Pharisees were gathered around xer, Jesus posed them a question, saying, How does it seem to you about the salve? whose xon is xe? They said to xer, The xon of David. Xe said to them, How is it then that David with breath calls xer boss, saying,

> The boss told my boss,
> Sit to my right,
>   until I put your enemies under your feet?

If David calls xer boss, how is xe his xon? No one was able to say a word in reply, and from that day on no one dared pose questions to xer.

Then Jesus spoke to the crowds and to xer apprentices, saying, The scribes and Pharisees sit in the seat of Moses, so do and observe all they tell you to, but don't do as they themselves do, because they don't do what they teach. They load others with burdensome loads that they themselves don't touch with even one of their fingers. All their works they perform in order to be seen by others: they make their phylacteries wide and their tassels long. They love the place of honor at feasts and front-row seats in the synagogues and deferential greetings in the town square and having others call them Rabbi. As for you, don't be called Rabbi, because you have one teacher, and you are all siblings. And don't call anyone on earth your fother because your one fother is in the sky. Don't call anyone guide, because your one guide is the salve. Among yourselves, let the servant be the greatest. Those who promote themselves will be humbled, and those who humble themselves will be promoted.

Oh you, scribes and Pharisees, you hypocrites, you close off the realm of the sky to humans: you yourselves don't enter, or allow those who would enter to go in: like dogs in a feed trough, you neither eat nor let the cows eat.

Oh you, scribes and Pharisees, you hypocrites, you cross sea and land to make a single convert, and then make that convert twice the child of Gehenna that you yourself are.

Oh you, blind guides who say, If someone swears by the sanctuary, it means nothing, but if someone swears by the gold of the sanctuary, it's binding. Blind morons, which is greater, the gold or the sanctuary that sacralizes the gold? You say, If someone swears by the altar, it means nothing, but if someone swears by the gift on the altar, it's binding. Blind ones, which is greater, the gift or the altar that sacralizes the gift? One who swears by the altar swears by it and by everything on it, and one who swears by the sanctuary swears by it and by xe who inhabits it, and one who swears by the sky swears by the throne of the god and by xe who is seated on it.

Oh you, scribes and Pharisees, you hypocrites, you tithe mint and dill and cumin, but you neglect weightier matters of the law:

fairness, mercy, and fidelity. These you should fulfill, without neglecting those others. Blind guides, you strain out the gnat but swallow the camel.

Oh you, scribes and Pharisees, you hypocrites, you clean the outside of the cup and the plate, but inside you yourselves are full of greed and double standards. Blind Pharisee, first clean the inside of the cup, so that the outside can become clean.

Oh you, scribes and Pharisees, you hypocrites, you resemble whitewashed tombs that on the outside look beautiful but inside are full of the bones of carcasses and all sorts of rot. Similarly, on the outside you present to others an appearance of justice, but inside you are full of hypocrisy and lawlessness.

Oh you, scribes and Pharisees, you hypocrites, you build tombs for the prophets and garnish the graves of the just, and declare, If we'd lived in the days of our fathers, we wouldn't have helped them shed the blood of the prophets. By this you testify against yourselves, that you are the sons of those who murdered the prophets. You fill to the brim the measuring cup your ancestors filled. You snakes, you knot of vipers, how will you escape the judgment of Gehenna? Because of this, look, I send you prophets and wise ones and writers, some of whom you kill and crucify, some of whom you whip in your synagogues, and chase from city to city, so that on you falls all the just blood shed on earth, from the blood of Abel the just to the blood of Zachariah son of Barachiah, whom you murdered between the sanctuary and the altar. Truly I tell you, all this falls on this generation.

Xe sat opposite the treasury and watched the crowd put money into the treasury. Many who were rich put in much. A poor widow came and put in two pennies, hardly worth a thing. Calling xer apprentices to xer, xe said to them, Truly I tell you, this poor widow has put more than any of the others into the treasury. All of them put in from their disposable wealth, but she in her dire need has put in all she had to live on.

As xe left the temple, one of xer apprentices said to xer, Teacher, look, what stones and what buildings! But Jesus replied, You see those gigantic buildings? Not one stone on a stone will go untoppled.

╬

Jesus went to the Mount of Olives. At dawn xe returned to the temple, and all the people came to xer, and xe sat and taught them. The scribes and Pharisees brought to xer a woman who'd been caught in adultery, and standing her front and center they challenged xer, Teacher, this woman was caught in the very act of adultery. In the law, Moses commands us to stone one like this. What do you say? They said this to test xer, to have some accusation against xer. Jesus squatted down and wrote with xer finger on the ground. When they kept asking xer, xe stood up and said to them, Let anyone among you who has never erred throw the first stone. And again xe squatted down and wrote on the ground. Hearing this, they went out, starting with the oldest and continuing to the last, leaving only Jesus and the woman where she stood. Jesus straightened back up and said to her, Woman, where are they? Did no one condemn you? She said, No one, boss. Jesus said, I don't condemn you, either. Go, and from now on shun errancy.

Again Jesus spoke to them, saying, I am the light of the world. One who follows me will not be journeying in darkness but will have the light of life. Why remain in darkness when you have access to light? Why drink murky water when you have access to clear? I am the beloved. I am the just. I am the xon of the fother. I speak, having heard. I command, having received the commandment. I reveal, having discovered. Look, I speak in order to exist. Listen to me, to see me. If I do exist, then who am I? I don't occur as I am, or appear as I am. The Pharisees said to xer, You're testifying about yourself; your testimony isn't true. Jesus replied and said to them, Even though I'm testifying about myself, my testimony is true because I know where I've come from and where I'm going. But you don't know where I've come from or where I'm going. You judge by the flesh; I don't judge anyone. But if I judge, my judgment is true, because I am not alone: we judge, I and the fother who sent me. In your own law it is written that the testimony of two persons is true. I testify about myself, and the fother who sent me testifies about me. They asked xer, Where's your fother? Jesus replied, You know neither me nor my fother; if you knew me, you would know my fother. Xe uttered these sayings in the treasury as xe taught in the temple, but no one arrested xer because xer hour had not come yet.

Again xe said to them, I'm going away, and you'll seek me, but you'll die in your error. Where I'm going, you can't come. The Jews asked, Surely xe won't kill xerself, even though xe's saying, Where I'm going, you can't come? And xe said to them, You're from below; I'm from above. You're of this world; I'm not of this world. That's why I told you you'll die in your errors: if you don't believe that I am, you will die in your errors. They asked xer, Who are you? Jesus said to them, What have I said from the beginning? I have much to say and judge about you, but the one who sent me is true, and what I hear from xer I declare to the world. They didn't understand that xe referred to the fother. Jesus continued, When you elevate the xon of humanity, then you will know that I am, and that I do nothing on my own, but what the fother has taught me, I speak. The one who sent me is with me: xe has not left me alone, because I always do what is pleasing to xer. To know the xon of humanity is to know oneself. This is wholeness of life, to know oneself in and of the whole.

I was assigned by the power. I am real to those who think me. I am found among those who seek me. Look at me, you who think on me; hear me, you who listen. You who wait for me, embrace me. Don't hide me from your sight, don't hate me with your voice or your hearing. Don't ignore me in any place, at any time. Be aware: don't ignore me.

I am the first and the last. I am the honored and the scorned. I am the whore and the chaste. I am the wife and the virgin. I am the mather and the daughter. I am the limbs of my mather. I am the sterile woman with many children. At my extravagant wedding I married no husband. I am the midwife and the one who helps at no birth. I am the comfort of labor pains. I am the bride and the groom, and I am conceived in my husband. I am my fother's mather and my husband's sister, and my husband is my child. I am the slave girl of the one who serves me. I am the ruler of my child. My child gave birth to me prematurely, my child who was born at the right time, my child who empowers me. . I am the staff of xer youthful authority, and xe is the cane for my old age. Xer wishes are my works. I am the silence that can't be comprehended, and the anticipation made of memory. I am the voice with many timbres and the word with many shapes. I am the assignment of my own name. I am knowledge and ignorance. I am timidity and boldness. I am shameless, I am ashamed. I am security and I am terror. I am war and peace.

Pay attention to me. I am the disgraced and the respected. Pay attention to my poverty and my wealth. Don't snub me when I've been knocked to the ground, and you will find me among those who rise up. Don't just stare at me on the dung heap, leaving me discarded there, and you will see me citizened in principalities. Don't just stare at me when I'm cast out among the outcasts, don't mock my extraordinary rendition to black sites. Don't throw me out among the genocided.

I am compassionate and I am cruel. Beware! Don't hate my obedience, don't love my self-determination. Don't take advantage of my weakness, don't fear my power.

Why do you despise my fear and curse my pride? I am xe who inhabits all fears, who gives strength through trembling. I am xe who is most timid when safe in a comfortable place. I am senseless and I am wise. Why have you excluded me from your considerations? By sharing silence with the silenced, I assert myself and speak out.

I, I am godless, and I am the one with the godliest god. I am the one you confess and the one you deny. I am unlearned, but you learn from me. I am the one you're dismissive of but can't forget. I am the one from whom you hide, to whom you appear. When you hide from me, I appear. When you appear, I hide from you.

I am the peace for which war is conducted. I am alien and citizen. I am being and nothingness: those who know me are me; those who don't are not. Those close to me don't know me; those far away do. On the day that I am nearby, you are far away; on the day that I am far from you, I am close to you.

I am restraint and the unrestrained. I am solution and dissolution. I am the perduring and the disintegrating. I have descended, so others ascend to me. I am conviction and acquittal. I am inerrant, and error grows from me. I am outward desire and inward self-control. I am spoken so that all hear but none understand. I am the unspeaking source of everything spoken. Hear me delicately, understand me roughly. I am xe who laments, face down in the dirt. I prepare my own bread, and my own mind. I know the known that the name names. I am xe who cries out and xe who hears the cry.

Hear me, listeners; learn from the words you already know. I am the heard that all can hear, the said that none can say. I am the name of the sound and the sound of the name. I am the sign of the signification that differs from difference. Look for my words in what has been written. Hear me, listeners, emissaries on assignment and breaths risen from the dead. I alone exist beyond judgment.

As xe was saying these things, many came to believe in xer.

Then Jesus said to the Jews who believed on xer, If you remain in my word, you will be truly my apprentices, and you will know the truth, and the truth will liberate you. They answered xer, We are Abraham's descendants and have never been enslaved by anyone; how dare you say, You will be liberated? Jesus answered them, Truly, truly I tell you, everyone who commits error is a slave of error. The slave does not belong to a household forever, but the xon does belong to it forever. So if the xon liberates you, you're liberated for real. I know you're descendants of Abraham, but you seek to kill me because my word has no place among you. I say what I have been shown by my fother, you do what you have heard from your father.

They answered and said to xer, Our father is Abraham. Jesus said to them, If you were the children of Abraham, you would do the works of Abraham. But now you seek to kill me, a person who tells you the truth xe heard from the god. Abraham didn't do that. Sure, you're doing the deeds of your father. They said to xer, We weren't born from fornication: we have one fother, the god. Jesus said to them, If the god were your fother, you would love me, because I came from the god and I've come here. I didn't come on my own, but xe sent me. Why do you not understand my sayings? Because you can't hear my word. You are from your father the devil, and you've chosen to do the will of your father. He was a murderer from the beginning, and can't stand the truth, because there is no truth in him. When he tells a lie, he speaks from his own nature, because he is a liar and the father of lies. I tell the truth, but you don't believe me. Who among you convicts me of error? If I tell the truth, why don't you believe me? One who is from the god hears the words of the god, but you don't hear them, because you're not from the god.

The Jews answered and said to xer, Are we not right to say you are a Samaritan and have a visitant? Jesus answered, I don't have a visitant, but I honor my father, and you dishonor me. I don't seek glory for myself; there is one who seeks and judges. Truly, truly I tell you, one who keeps my word will not see death, ever. The Jews said to xer, Now we know you have a visitant. Abraham and the prophets are dead, yet you say, One who keeps my word will not see death, ever. Are you greater than our father Abraham, who is dead? And the prophets are dead. Who do you make yourself out to be? Jesus replied, If I glorify myself, my glory is nothing. It is my father who glorifies me, the one of whom you say xe is our god. You have not known xer, but I know xer, and if I said I didn't know xer, I'd be a liar like you, but I do know xer, and I keep xer word. Your father Abraham looked forward to seeing my day, and he saw it and was glad. The Jews said to xer, You're not fifty years old, and you've seen Abraham? Jesus said to them, Truly, truly I tell you, before Abraham was born, I am. They picked up stones to throw at xer, but Jesus hid, and left the temple.

Xe was sitting on the Mount of Olives facing the temple, and Peter and James and John and Andrew asked xer privately, Tell us, when will these things happen, and what will be the sign that all these things are about to be accomplished? Jesus answered, telling them, Watch out, so that no one misleads you. Many will come in my name claiming, I am xe, and will mislead many. When you hear of wars and rumors of wars, don't fret; such things must happen, but they're not the end. People will rise against people, and realm against realm, and there will be earthquakes all over the place, and there will be famines. These are the beginning of sorrows.

Watch out for yourselves; they will hand you over to courts, and you will be beaten in synagogues, and you will stand before governors and kings for my sake, as witnesses to them. But first the good news must be declared to all peoples. When they arrest you and bring you to trial, don't worry what you'll say, but whatever is given you in the moment, say that, because it will not be you speaking, but the holy breath. Brother will betray brother to death, and father child, and children will rise up against parents and put them to death, and you will be hated by all because of my name. The one who perseveres to the end will be preserved.

If they say to you, Look, xe is in the desert, don't go out there; Look, xe is in the inner rooms, don't believe it. Like lightning that, flashing in the east, is seen all the way to the west, so will be the coming of the xon of humanity.

But in those days, after that oppression,

The sun will go dark,

and the moon will not give its light,

and the stars will fall from the sky,

and the powers in the skies will be shaken,

and then they will see the xon of humanity coming on the clouds with great power and glory. And then xe will send the emissaries and gather the chosen from the four winds, from the reaches of the earth, from the reaches of the skies.

Now learn from a parable about the fig tree. When its branches soften and send out shoots, you know summer is near. In the same way, when you see these things happening, you will know xe is near, right at the door. Truly I tell you, this generation will not depart until all these things have happened. The sky and the earth will pass by, but my words will not pass by. About that day and hour no one knows, not the emissaries in the sky, not the xon, only the fother.

Xer apprentices asked xer, When will the realm arrive? Jesus replied, It will not arrive because of expectation. No one will tell you, Look, here it is, or Look, there it is. Instead, the realm of the fother is spread across the earth already, and people don't recognize it.

Take care that your hearts not turn torpid from partying, drunkenness, and the worries of life, and that day catch you unexpectedly like a trap, because it will close over everyone on the whole face of the earth. Be alert at all times, praying that you will have the stamina to outlast all these things that will happen, and stand before the xon of humanity.

During the day xe was teaching in the temple, but at night xe would go out and stay on the hill called the Mount of Olives. And all the people rose early in the morning to hear xer in the temple.

The realm of the skies resembles ten bridesmaids who, taking lanterns with them, went out to welcome the groom. Five of them were careless, five prudent. The careless ones took their lanterns with them, but didn't take oil; the prudent ones brought flasks of oil along with their lanterns. It took a while for the groom to arrive, and they all got drowsy and nodded off. In the middle of the night came the cry, Look, the groom: go out for the greeting. Then all the bridesmaids got up and trimmed their lanterns, and the careless ones said to the prudent, Give us some of your oil; our lanterns are going out. But the prudent ones replied, No, there's not enough for us and you; go to the merchants and buy some for yourselves. While they were off shopping, the groom arrived, and the ones who'd been ready went with him to the wedding feast, and the door was shut. Later the other bridesmaids arrived, saying, Boss, boss, open up. But in reply he said, Truly I tell you, I don't know you. So keep watch, because you don't know the day or the hour.

It's as if a man going on a journey called together his slaves and entrusted to them his holdings. To one he gave five thousand, to another two, and to another one, to each according to his ability, and he took off. The one who had received five thousand went and traded on it, and made five thousand more. Similarly, the one who had received two thousand made two thousand from it. But the one who had received one thousand dug a hole in the ground and hid his boss's money. After a long time, the boss of those slaves returned, and settled accounts with them. The one who had received five thousand came forward with the additional five thousand, saying, Boss, you gave me five thousand; look, I've made five thousand more.

The boss said to him, Well done, good and faithful slave, you've been faithful with a little so I'll put you in charge of a lot. You're in the good graces of your boss. The one who had received the two thousand came forward and said, Boss, you gave me two thousand; look, I've made two thousand more. The boss said to him, Well done, good and faithful slave, you've been faithful with a little so I'll put you in charge of a lot. You're in the good graces of your boss. The one who had received one thousand came forward and said, boss, I knew that you're a hard man, harvesting what you didn't plant and gathering what you didn't scatter, so from fear I went and hid your thousand in the ground. Look, you have what is yours. In reply the boss said to him, You clumsy, lazy slave, you knew that I harvest what I didn't plant and gather what I didn't scatter? Then at least you should have put my money in the bank, so that on my return I'd have gotten it back with interest. Take the thousand from him and give it to the one with ten thousand. To all who have, more will be given, and they'll be flush, but from one who has little, even what he has will be taken away. Toss this worthless slave into outer darkness, where there will be weeping and grinding of teeth.

When the xon of humanity comes in xer glory, and all the emissaries with xer, then xe'll sit in glory on xer throne, and before xer all peoples will be assembled, and xe will separate them from one another the way a shepherd separates sheep from goats, and xe'll set the sheep on xer right and the goats on xer left. Then the ruler will say to those on xer right, Come, you who have been blessed by my fother, inherit the realm prepared for you from the foundation of the world. I was hungry and you gave me to eat, I was thirsty and you gave me to drink, I was a foreigner and you welcomed me, naked and you clothed me, sick and you attended me, in prison and you visited me. Then the just will answer xer, saying, Boss, when did we see you hungry and feed you, or thirsty and give you to drink? When did we see you a foreigner and welcome you, or naked and clothe you? When did we see you sick or in prison and visit you? And in reply the ruler will say to them, Truly I tell you, anything you did for the least of these my siblings, you did for me.

Then xe'll say to those on xer left, Go away from me, cursed ones, into the timeless fire prepared for the devil and his emissaries. I was hungry and you did not give me to eat, I was thirsty and you did not give me to drink, I was a foreigner and you did not welcome me, naked and you did not clothe me, sick and in prison and you did not visit me. Then in reply they'll say to xer, Boss, when did we see you hungry or thirsty or naked or sick or in prison, and didn't tend to you? Xe'll reply, saying, Truly I tell you, anything you didn't do for the least of these, you didn't do for me. And these will go off to timeless punishment, but the just to timeless life.

Going along, xe saw a blind man. Xer apprentices inquired, saying, Rabbi, who erred, him or his parents, for him to be born blind? Jesus answered, Neither he nor his parents erred; it was so that the works of the god would be displayed in him. I work the works of the one who sent me while it's daytime; night is coming, when no one will be able to work. While I am in the world, I am the light of the world. When xe'd said this xe spat on the ground and made mud with the spit and smeared the mud on the man's eyes and told him, Go wash in the pool of Siloam (which translates to Sent). He went and washed, and returned with sight. The neighbors and those who before had seen him begging said, Isn't this the one who used to sit and beg? Some said, It's him, but others said, No, it's someone like him. But he said, It's me. They asked him, How were your eyes opened? He answered them, The person named Jesus made mud and smeared it on my eyes and told me, Go wash in Siloam. I went, and once I'd washed I could see. They asked him, Where is xe? He said, I don't know.

They led before the Pharisees the one who had been blind. It had been a sabbath day when Jesus made the mud and opened his eyes. Again the Pharisees questioned him about how he had received his sight. He told them, Xe put mud on my eyes, and I washed, and now I see. Some of the Pharisees said, This person is not from the god, because xe does not keep the sabbath. Others said,

How could a person who is an errant perform such signs? So there was division among them. They spoke again to the blind man, What do *you* say about xer who opened your eyes? He said, Xe is a prophet. But the Jews did not believe that he had been blind and then received his sight, until they summoned the parents of the man who had received his sight, and asked them, saying, Is this your son, the one you say was born blind? How does he now see? His parents answered them and said, We know that this is our son and that he was born blind. How he now can see we don't know, and who has opened his eyes we don't know. Ask him: he is of age, and can speak for himself. His parents said this because they feared the Jews, because the Jews had already agreed that anyone who acknowledged xer as the salve would be put out of the synagogue. For this reason, his parents said, He is of age, ask him.

So for a second time they summoned the man who had been blind, and said to him, Give glory to the god; we know this person is an errant. He answered, I don't know whether he is an errant. One thing I do know: I was blind, but now I see. They asked him, What did xe do to you? How did xe open your eyes? He answered them, I told you already, but you didn't listen. Why do you want to hear it again? You don't want to become xer apprentices, do you? They insulted him and said, You are xer apprentice; we are apprentices of Moses. We know that the god spoke to Moses, but we don't know where this person is coming from. In reply the man said to them, This is an amazing thing, that you don't know where this person is coming from, but xe opened my eyes. We know that the god does not listen to errants, but does listen to the god-fearing who do xer will. From the beginning of time it's unheard of that someone opened the eyes of the blind; if this person were not of the god, xe could do no such thing. In reply they said to him, You've been in error even from birth, and *you're* teaching *us*? And they threw him out.

Jesus heard they'd thrown him out, and found him and asked him, Do you believe in the xon of humanity? He said in reply, Who is xe, boss, so that I may believe in xer? Jesus told him, You have seen xer, and the one you are speaking with now is xer. He said, I believe, boss. And he worshiped xer. Jesus said, I have come into the world for judgment, so that those who *don't* see *do* see, and those who see become blind.

Some of the Pharisees who were nearby heard this and asked xer, Surely we're not blind, are we? Jesus told them, If you were blind, you wouldn't be in error, but now, because you say, We see, your error remains. It is as impossible to look at the salve as at the sun. The god looks at everyone; no one looks at the god. The salve ungrudgingly receives and gives. The salve is the light of the fother, giving light freely, shining light everywhere.

Truly, truly I tell you, the one who doesn't enter the sheep pen through the gate but sneaks into it some other way is a thief, a rustler. The one who enters through the gate is the shepherd of those sheep. The person on watch opens the gate for xer, and the sheep hear xer voice, and xe calls them by name and leads them out. When xe has herded out all of xer own, xe leads the way ahead of them and they follow because they know xer voice. They won't follow a stranger, but will run from him, because they don't know the stranger's voice. Jesus spoke to them in this figurative way, but they didn't understand what xe was saying to them.

Again Jesus said, Truly, truly I tell you that I am the gate for the sheep. All who came before me were thieves and rustlers, and the sheep didn't listen to them. I am the gate: whoever enters through me will be preserved, and will come in and go out, and find pasture. The thief comes only to steal and kill and destroy; I have come so that they may have life, and have it more fully. I am the good shepherd. The good shepherd devotes xer soul to the sheep. The hired hand (who isn't the shepherd and these aren't his own sheep) sees a wolf coming and deserts the flock and runs away, and the wolf preys on the sheep and scatters them. The hired hand runs away because he's just a hired hand and doesn't care about the sheep. I am the good shepherd, and I know my own, and my own know me, just as I know the fother and the fother knows me, and I devote my soul to the sheep. I have other sheep that are not in this pen; I must bring them, too. They will listen to my voice and there will be one flock, one shepherd. My fother loves me because I devote my soul to the sheep, so that I can claim it back. No one takes it from me; I devote it on my own. I have authority to offer it, and I have authority to claim it again. I have received this charge from my fother. I am the gateway to life. The one who enters through me enters into life.

Jesus cried out and said, One who believes in me believes not in me but in the one who sent me. And one who sees me sees the one who sent me. I have come, a light to the world, so that all who believe in me will not remain in darkness. If someone hears my sayings and does not keep them, I don't judge that person, because I came not to judge the world but to preserve the world. The one who rejects me and does not receive my sayings has a judge: the word I have said will judge that person on the last day of the world. I have not spoken on my own, but the fother who sent me gave me a command, what to say and sing. And I know that xer command is timeless life. What I say, I say exactly as the fother said it to me.

I, the perfect forethought of everything, transformed myself into my offspring. I got here first, blazing every trail. I am the luminosity of light, the memory of the here and now. I entered the domain of darkness and continued through to its central prison. The foundations of chaos shook, but I hid myself from the harmful ones, so they couldn't recognize me. I came out of hiding, and continued on, light from those who live in light, the memory of forethought.

I reached the center of the darkness, the inside of the below, to fulfill my mission. The foundations of chaos shook, threatening to collapse onto those trapped in chaos, destroying them, but I secured them with the roots of my light, to prevent their being destroyed too soon. I am the light-lit light, the memory of forethought, able to penetrate the center of the darkness, the inside of the below.

My face shone with light that overcame that domain, and I broke into their prison, the prison of the body, and declared, Hear this, and awaken from your deep sleep. The hearer wept, and wiping away the tears asked, Who is calling my name? Where has hope arrived from, to me in my imprisonment? I replied, I am the forethought of pure light, the thought of the virgin breath, raising you up to a place of honor. Stand up, remember what you have heard, and trace your roots to me, the merciful. Guard yourself against the emissaries of impoverishment, and the visitants of chaos, and all who try to trap you. Beware of the deep sleep, the confinement to the inside of the below.

I raised up the hearer. I locked the hearer in liquid light with five locks, so death from then on could not break in.

Division occurred again among the Jews over these words. Many of them said, Xe has a visitant, and is raving. Why listen to xer? Others said, These aren't the words of one who is visited. Can a visitant open the eyes of a blind person?

⧻

The feast of dedication was taking place then in Jerusalem; it was winter, and Jesus was walking in the temple, through the porch of Solomon. The Jews gathered around xer and said to xer, How long will you keep our souls in suspense? If you are the salve, tell us plainly. Jesus answered them, I told you but you didn't believe: the works that I do in the name of my fother attest to me, but you didn't believe, because you are not my sheep. My sheep hear my voice, and I know them and they follow me, and I give them time-less life and they will not pass away and no one can snatch them from my hand. My fother who gave them to me is greater than all else, and no one can snatch them from the hand of the fother. I and the fother are one.

Again the Jews picked up stones, to stone xer. Jesus answered them, I have shown you many good works from the fother; for which of those works are you stoning me? The Jews answered xer, We're not stoning you for a good work but for blasphemy, that you, a human, pretend to be a god. Jesus answered them, Is it not written in your law, I said, you are gods? If those to whom the word of the god was given are gods, and the writing cannot be faulted, do you say the one the fother sanctified and sent into the world blasphemes because I said I am the xon of the god? If I don't do the works of my fother, don't believe me, but if I do, even if you don't believe me, believe the works, so that you will know and under-stand that the fother is in me and I am in the fother. Learn who the salve is, and win xer as a friend, because xe is a true friend. Xe is also a god and a teacher. Xe, being divine, became human for your sake. Xe breaks the iron bars and bronze bolts of the underworld. Xe resists and overthrows every arrogant tyrant. Xe escapes any chains in which xe is bound. Xe releases the poor from the abyss and the mourners from the underworld. Xe humbles those made proud by power, putting to shame their arrogance. Xer weakness overwhelms the strong and boastful, and xer meekness disproves the assertive, valorizing humility before the god. Having assumed humanity, xe is the patience with humanity of the god, the indulgence toward humanity of the divine word. Xe restores humility to the celebrated. The one who gives humanity to humanity assumed humanity not to install humanity in the god but install divinity in the human. Again they sought to arrest xer, but xe eluded their grasp.

There were some Greeks among those who had come up to worship at the festival. They came to Philip, who was from Bethsaida in Galilee, and asked him, saying, Boss, we want to see Jesus. Philip came and told Andrew; Andrew and Philip came and told Jesus. Jesus answered them, saying, The hour has come for the xon of humanity to be glorified. Truly, truly I tell you, if a kernel of wheat does not fall to the ground and die, it remains alone. But if it dies, it yields much grain. The one who loves her soul will lose it, but the one who hates her soul in this world protects it for timeless life. If anyone would serve me, follow me, and wherever I am my servant too will be. The fother will honor whoever serves me.

But now my soul is troubled. What should I say? Fother, preserve me from this hour? But it was for this that I came to this hour. Fother, glorify your name. A voice came from the sky, I have glorified it, and will glorify it again. Some who stood there and heard it said it was thunder. Others said, An emissary has spoken for xer. In answer, Jesus said, The voice came not for me but for you. Now is the judgment of this world, now the principal of this world will be expelled. If I am lifted up from the earth, I will draw everyone to myself. Xe said this to indicate what kind of death xe would die. The crowd answered xer, We have heard from the law that the salve will remain forever. How can you say that the xon of humanity will be lifted up? Who is this xon of humanity? Jesus said to them, The light is with you only for a short time. Walk while you have the light, so that darkness not catch you. If you walk in darkness, you don't know where you're going. While you have the light, believe in

the light, so that you may become children of light. Light and darkness, life and death, right and left are siblings, inseparable. Because
of this, the good are not good, the bad are not bad, life is not life,
death is not death. Each dissolves into its generating source, but
what transcends the world is indissoluble and timeless.

Jesus said these things, then went away and hid from them.
Even though xe had performed many signs in their presence, they
didn't believe in xer, so that the word spoken by the prophet Isaiah
would be fulfilled,

> Boss, who has believed our message,
>> and to whom has the arm of the boss been shown?

For this reason they could not believe, because, as Isaiah also
says,

> Xe has blinded their eyes
>> and blocked their heart,
> so that they neither see with their eyes
>> nor know in their heart and turn
> to let me heal them.

Isaiah said these things, because he saw xer glory and sang of xer.
Still, many, even of the principals, believed in xer, though the
Pharisees did not admit it openly, so as not to be kicked out of the
synagogue, because they preferred glory from humans to the glory
from the god.

Again xe went away, beyond the Jordan, to the place where
John first baptized, and remained there. And many came to xer,
and they said, John performed no signs, but everything he said
about this person proved true. And many believed in xer there.

Lazarus of Bethany, the brother of Mary and Martha, fell ill,
so the sisters sent to xer, saying Boss, look, the one you love is ill.
Hearing this, Jesus said, This illness isn't terminal, but for the glory
of the god, so that by it the xon of the god may be glorified. Jesus
loved Martha and her sister and Lazarus, so, hearing that he was
ill, xe stayed two days in the same place, but after that said to xer
apprentices, Let's go back to Judea. The apprentices said to xer,
Rabbi, the Judeans were trying just now to stone you, and you're
going back? Jesus replied, Are there not twelve hours of daytime?
One who walks in the day doesn't stumble, but sees by the light of

this world. But one who walks at night stumbles because there is no light for him. The principals cannot see those immersed in perfect light, or detain them. Xe said this, and then said to them, Our friend Lazarus is sleeping, but we go so I can awaken him. Jesus referred to his death, but they thought xe only meant resting sleep, so Jesus said plainly, Lazarus has died. I'm glad, for the sake of your faith, that I wasn't there, but now let's go to him. Xe said to Thomas, the one whose fellow apprentices called him the Twin, Let's go, so that we can die with him.

Arriving, Jesus found that Lazarus had been in the tomb for four days already. Bethany was near Jerusalem, only a couple of miles away, and many Judeans had come to Martha and Mary to console them about their brother. When Martha heard Jesus was coming, she went to meet xer while Mary stayed at home. Martha said to Jesus, Boss, if you'd been here, my brother wouldn't have died, but I know that even now anything you ask for from the god, the god will give you. Jesus said to her, Your brother will stand back up. Martha said to xer, I know that he will stand up in the standing up on the last day. Jesus said to her, I am the standing up and the life. All who live and believe on me will not die, ever. Do you believe this? She said to xer, Yes, boss, I have believed that you are the salve, the xon of the god, the one who has come into the world.

Having declared this, she went back and called her sister Mary, telling her in private, The teacher is here and calling for you. When she heard that, she got up quickly and went to xer. Jesus had not yet reached the village, but was still at the place where Martha had met xer. The Judeans who were with her at the house comforting her, seeing Mary stand up suddenly and go out, followed her, thinking she was going to the tomb to weep there. When Mary got to where Jesus was and saw xer, she fell at xer feet, saying to xer, Boss, if you'd been here, my brother wouldn't have died. When Jesus saw her weeping, and the Judeans who'd come with her weeping, xe groaned in breath, much troubled, and asked, Where have you laid him? They said to xer, Boss, come and see. Jesus wept, and the Judeans said, Look how xe loved him. But some of them said, Couldn't one who opened the eyes of a blind person have prevented this man's death?

Jesus, again groaning to xerself, came to the tomb. It was a cave with a stone against it. Jesus said, Take away the stone. Martha, the dead man's sister, said to xer, Boss it's been four days, there'll be a stench. Jesus said to her, Didn't I tell you that if you believe you will see the glory of the god? So they moved the stone. Jesus turned xer eyes upward and said, Fother, I thank you that you have heard me. I know that you always hear me, but because of the crowd standing here I say so, so that they will believe that you sent me. Having said this, xe cried in a loud voice, Lazarus, come out. The dead man came out, his feet and hands wound with rags and his face covered with a cloth. Jesus told them, Unwrap him, and let him go.

Many of the Judeans who had come to Mary and had seen what xe did believed on xer, but some went to the Pharisees and told them what Jesus had done. The chief priests and the Pharisees convened in the council and said, What should we do about this person who is performing so many signs? If we let xer keep on like this, everyone will believe on xer, and the Romans will come and destroy our place and our clan. One of them, Caiaphas, chief priest that year, said to them, You don't get it. You haven't figured out that it's better for you to have one person die for the rest than that the whole clan perish. He didn't say this on his own, but as high priest that year he prophesied that Jesus would die for the people, and not only for the one clan but to gather into one the dispersed children of the god. From that day on, they plotted how to kill xer.

So Jesus no longer walked openly among the Jews, but went out to a stretch near the desert, to a town called Ephraim, and remained there with the apprentices.

Before xe was arrested, Jesus gathered xer apprentices together and said, Before I'm offered up to them, let's sing a hymn to the fother, and then go out to what awaits us. Xe had them form a circle, holding hands, and xe xerself stood in the middle. Xe said, Respond Amen to me. Then xe started singing the hymn, intoning, Glory to you, the fother. Those encircling xer replied, Amen.

Glory to you, the word. Glory to you, grace. Amen.
Glory to you, breath. Glory to you, the holy. Glory to

your glory. Amen.

We praise you, the fother. We give you thanks, light in
whom no darkness dwells. Amen.

It gives thanks from us for me to declare:

I am preserved, and I preserve. Amen.

I am released, and I release. Amen.

I am pierced, and I pierce. Amen.

I am born, and I give birth. Amen.

I eat, and I am eaten. Amen.

I hear, and I am heard. Amen.

I understand; I am understanding. Amen.

I am washed, and I wash. Amen.

    Grace dances.

I play the flute, you dance. Amen.

I mourn, you lament. Amen.

An octet sings backup for us. Amen.

The number twelve dances above us. Amen.

The whole cosmos joins in our dancing. Amen.

One who does not dance does not know what is happening.
Amen.

I depart, and I stay. Amen.

I adorn, and I am adorned. Amen.

I am united, and I unite. Amen.

I am homeless, and I have homes. Amen.

I am placeless, and I am placed. Amen.

I am templeless, and I have temples. Amen.

I am a lamp to you who see me. Amen.

I am a mirror to you who recognize me. Amen.

I am a door to you who knock. Amen.

I am a road for you, traveler. Amen.

If you follow my dancing, see yourself in me when I speak;
if you have observed my deeds, keep silent about my mysteries.
You who dance, watch what I do, because yours is the passion of
humanity I am to suffer. You couldn't understand what you suffer,
had I the word not been sent to you by the fother. When you see
me suffer, you see suffering itself; seeing it, you are not indifferent
but deeply moved. Building toward wisdom, you have me for

foundation. Rest on me. Who I am, you will know only after I leave. I am not what I am now seen to be. You will see as you approach. If you knew how to suffer, you would be able not to suffer; learn to suffer, and you will be able not to suffer. What you don't know, I'll teach you. I am your god, not the betrayer's. I will holy souls into harmony with me. Learn the word of wisdom. Sing again with me:

Glory to you, the fother.
Glory to you, the word.
Glory to you, breath.

If you want to know about me: as the word, I once dumb-founded everything, and was not in the least shy about it. I leaped. Understand wholeness. Having understood, sing,

Glory to you, the fother. Amen.

After this dance, beloved, the boss departed, and the apprentices, like sleepwalkers, dispersed.

The Passover of the Jews was near, and many traveled from the countryside into Jerusalem before Passover to purify themselves. They searched for Jesus, and said to one another as they stood in the temple, How does it seem to you? Surely xe won't come to the feast, will xe? The chief priests and the Pharisees had issued an edict that anyone who knew where Jesus was should tell, so they could arrest xer.

╬

Here is the secret word that Jesus revealed to Judas in the course of a week, three days before xe celebrated Passover. When xe appeared on earth, Jesus performed signs and great wonders for the saving of humanity. Since some humans walked the path of justice but others wandered errantly, xe called twelve apprentices, with whom xe spoke about mysteries and inevitabilities. Often instead of appearing to xer apprentices as xerself, xe presented xerself among them as a child.

One day in Judea, Jesus went to xer apprentices, arriving while they were gathered together reverently. Xe approached while they were seated, giving thanks over the bread. Xe laughed. The apprentices asked xer, Teacher, why are you laughing at us for giving thanks? What's wrong with that? We're doing the right thing. In answer xe said to them, I'm not laughing at you, not for doing this thing that, rather than acting out your desires, gives your god praise. They replied, Teacher, you are the xon of our god. Jesus challenged them, How do you know me? Truly I tell you, no one from the generation represented here will know me.

When xer apprentices heard this, they grew angry and resentful, and began in their hearts to excoriate xer. Jesus, recognizing their lack of understanding, asked them, Why has a little pushback provoked such hostility in you? The irritation in your souls irritates your god who is within you. If you're so strong, produce a perfect human and stand that person here in front of me. They all protested, We are strong. But none of them had breath enough to stand up to Jesus, except for Judas Iscariot. He was able to stand before xer, though even he couldn't look xer in the eye, but had to turn his face away. Judas said to xer, I know who you are and where you have come from. You come from the immortal realm, and I am not worthy to utter the name of the one who has sent you.

Jesus, recognizing that Judas' mind was turned toward lofty matters, beckoned him, Step here away from the others and I'll tell you the mysteries of the realm, not so that you will go there, but to fill out your grief. Someone else will replace you to keep the twelve untroubled toward their god. Judas asked xer, When will you tell me these things? On what generation will the day of bright light dawn? But he hadn't finished speaking before Jesus left.

The morning after this, Jesus appeared again to xer apprentices, who asked xer, Teacher, where did you go and what did you do when you left us? Jesus told them, I went to a different generation, a great and holy one. Xer apprentices asked, What generation is so much greater and holier than ours, but not visible to us here? Hearing this, Jesus laughed, and said to them, Why worry yourselves over the strong and holy generation? Truly I tell you, no one born in this age will see that generation, and no host of emissaries from the stars will rule over that generation, and no human of mortal birth will be able to join it. That generation will not submit to the authorities you recognize. Jesus said: If, as your authority figures insist, the realm is in the sky, then the birds of the sky precede you. If, as they say, it is in the sea, then the fish precede you. But the realm is inside you and it is outside you. Once you know yourselves, you will be known, and you will recognize yourselves as children of the living fother, but until you know yourselves you live in poverty, you are poverty. When xer apprentices heard this, they were upset, and could find nothing to say.

On another day, Jesus visited them again. They told xer, Teacher, we've seen you in a vision; we had vivid dreams last night. Xe asked them, Why have you gone into hiding? They answered, We have seen a giant house, and in it a huge altar with twelve men around it, priests, repeating a name. A crowd that included us was waiting for the priests to present the offerings. Jesus asked them, What were the priests like? They replied, Some fast for two weeks, some sacrifice their own children and their wives, in a contest of praise and blame. Some murder, others commit various other acts of errant lawlessness. But around the altar they all invoke your name, acting out enough sacrifices to fill the altar.

After saying this, they grew troubled, and fell silent. Jesus asked them, Why are you so troubled? Truly I tell you, all the priests at that altar invoke my name, but the trees they plant bear no fruit. Jesus went on, You are the ones presenting offerings at the altar you have seen. That god is the god you serve, and the twelve men you have seen are you. The cattle brought in are the many people sacrificed, the crowd that, leading it toward that altar, you lead astray. The principal of this world in rising to power will make use of my name like this, and generations of pious people will follow him. After him, another will rise to power from the promiscuous, another from the child-murderers, and yet others from people of other forms of corruption, lawlessness, and error, declaring themselves like emissaries but proving to be the stars that bring everything to its end. Across the generations it has been declared, Look, the god has accepted your sacrifice from the hands of the priests. But they are promulgators of error. The boss who made the rules will enforce them, ultimately putting these others to shame. This boss waters the paradise of the god, not for one generation but to all timelessness.

Judas asked xer, Teacher, what fruit does this generation produce? Jesus replied, Generations replace one another, but in the time of the realm when a body dies breath leaves it but a soul lives on and is taken up. Judas asked, What will later human generations do? Jesus said, It is impossible to sow seed on rock and get grain from it, as the polluted nation in its corrupted wisdom tries to do. No emissary or officer now can envision the realm that the great holy generation will see.

Judas said, Teacher, you've listened to all of them, now listen to me, because I've seen a great vision. Hearing this, Jesus laughed and said, Thirteenth visitant, why are you so insistent? Go ahead and speak: I'll hear you out. Judas told xer, In the vision I saw the twelve apprentices stoning me in furious persecution, but afterward I reached the place where you were, a house bigger than my eyes could take in. A big crowd surrounded it, and it had a thatched roof. Inside the house, too, was a big crowd, and I begged, Teacher, let me in to join them. In reply, Jesus said, Judas, your star has led you to err. Xe continued, No person of mortal birth is worthy to enter the house you have seen, which is reserved for the holy. Sun and moon do not govern it; the holy emissaries dwell there not through days but across timelessness. Look, I'm telling you the mysteries of the realm, warning you of the errors of the stars.

Judas said, Teacher, maybe my seed, too, is subject to these principals? Jesus warned him, You will grieve when you see past your generation to the realm. When Judas heard this, he objected, What good can I hope for, since you've separated me from my generation? Jesus replied, You will become the thirteenth, to be cursed by the very generations you govern, never ascending into the holy generation.

Jesus said, Come, I will teach you about what no human has seen. There exists a vast, limitless realm the extent of which not even emissaries can measure, inhabited by an infinite, invisible breath that not even an emissary's eye can see, and that no mind can comprehend, no name can designate. A luminous cloud appeared there, and it said, Let there be an emissary, as my attendant. And from the cloud emerged a potent emissary, the self-generative, the god of light, because of whom four other emissaries emerged from another cloud, as attendants for the self-generative. And the self-generative said, Let Adamas come to exist, and Adamas existed. And it created the first luminary to rule over him. And it said, Let emissaries come to exist to serve him, and countless myriads existed. And it said, Let a lasting light source come to exist, and it existed. Then it created the second luminary to rule over it, and countless emissaries to attend it. This is how it created the rest of the lasting lights and gave them their authority, and provided emissaries to attend them. What we call the cosmos consists of that congregation of immortals.

Then Judas asked Jesus, How long will humanity exist? Jesus replied, Why fret that? Adam and his lineage live a duration determined by number in an order governed by it. Adam came from power and wealth, but proved unworthy. Had he been worthy, he would not have tasted death.

Judas asked Jesus, Does the human breath die? Jesus replied, That is why the god gave Michael to apportion people breaths only for service, but the great one gave Gabriel to complement breath with unconstrained soul, installed in the flesh by the generations of emissaries. Thus the god gave Adam and those after him knowledge, to exempt humans from subjection to the rulers of chaos and the underworld. Look, I've told you enough. Turn your eyes upward and observe the cloud and the light from it and the stars around it. The star that leads the way is your star. So Judas turned his eyes upward and observed the luminous cloud and entered it.

It was two days before Passover and the Feast of Unleavened Bread, and the chief priests and scribes were looking for some way to take xer by surprise and kill xer. But they said, Not during the feast, when there might be a riot from the people.

When xe was in Bethany at the house of Simon the leprous, while xe was reclining at the table a woman came with an alabaster jar of very expensive oil, genuine spikenard, and opened the jar and poured the oil on xer head. Some muttered to one another in indignation, Why waste the oil in this way? It could have been sold for three hundred bucks and the money given to the poor. They scolded her. But Jesus said, Leave her be; why are you hassling her? She has done me a good deed. You'll always have the poor among you, and you can do good for them any time you want, but you won't always have me. She has done what she could: she has anointed my body before the burial. Truly I tell you, wherever in the whole world the good news is declared, what she has done will be recounted in memory of her.

Then Judas Iscariot, one of the twelve, went to the chief priests, to betray xer to them. Hearing it, they were glad, and promised to give him a reward. He sought an opportunity to betray xer.

⚏

On the first day of the Feast of Unleavened Bread, when the passover lamb is sacrificed, xer apprentices said to xer, Where do you want us to go, to prepare the passover lamb for you to eat? So xe sent two of xer apprentices and said to them, Go into the city, and a man carrying a water jug will meet you. Follow him, and wherever he enters, say to the householder, The teacher asks, Where is my guest room, where I with my apprentices may eat the passover lamb? He'll show you a large upper room, furnished and ready. Prepare for us there. So the apprentices left and went into the city and found just what xe'd said and prepared the passover meal.

When evening came, xe arrived with the twelve. While they were reclining and eating, Jesus said, Truly I tell you that one of you who is eating with me will betray me. They were upset, and one by one asked xer, Not me? Xe said to them, One of the twelve who soaks bread in the bowl with me. The xon of humanity goes away, as it is written about xer, but oh the human by whom the xon of humanity is betrayed. Better for him that he'd never been born.

While they were eating, Jesus took bread and blessed it and broke it and gave it to the apprentices and said, Take, eat, this is my body. Taking the cup, xe gave thanks and gave it to them, saying, Drink from this, all of you, because this is my blood of the bequest, that is poured out for many for the sending away of errors. I tell you, I won't drink this fruit of the vine again until that day when I drink fresh wine with you in the realm of my fother.

Jesus told them, You'll all stumble, as is written,

    I will strike the shepherd,

        and the sheep will be scattered.

But after I am raised up I will go ahead of you into Galilee. Peter said to xer, They'll all stumble, but I won't. Jesus told him, Truly I tell you, this day, this very night, before the cock crows twice you will disavow me three times. He declared vehemently, Even if I have to die with you, I won't disavow you. They all spoke in the same way.

When supper was over, the devil having put into the heart of Judas the son of Simon the Iscariot to betray xer, knowing that the fother had given all things into xer hands, and the xe came from god and was returning to the god, xe rose from supper and took off xer cloak and took a towel and tied it around xer waist. Then xe poured water into a basin and began to wash the feet of the apprentices and to dry them with the towel around xer waist. Xe came to Simon Peter, who said to xer, Boss, do you mean to wash my feet? In answer Jesus said to him, You don't understand now what I'm doing, but later you will. Peter said to xer, You'll never wash my feet. Jesus answered him, If I don't wash you, you have no part with me. So Simon Peter said to xer, Boss, don't wash only my feet, then, but also my hands and head. Jesus told him, One who has bathed need not wash up except for his feet, because he is clean all over, and you are clean, but not all of you. Because xe knew who would betray xer. Because of this, xe said, Not all of you are clean.

When xe had washed their feet and put on xer cloak and reclined again, xe asked them, Do you get what I have done for you? You call me the teacher and the boss, and you speak well, because I am. If I, the boss and the teacher, wash your feet, you should wash one another's feet. I've given you an example; you should do as I have done. Truly, truly I tell you, the servant is not greater than the boss, nor the sent than the sender. Knowing these things, you're graceful if you do them. I don't speak about all of you: I know which ones I've chosen. But this is to fulfill the writing, *The one who ate my bread has turned his heel to me.* I tell you this before it happens, so that when it happens you will believe that I am. Truly,

truly I tell you, whoever receives someone I send receives me, and whoever receives me receives the one who sent me.

Having said these things, Jesus, troubled in breath, testified and said, Truly, truly I tell you that one of you will betray me. The apprentices looked at one another, unsure which of them xe meant. One of the apprentices, the one Jesus loved, was reclining against xer breast, so Simon Peter gestured to him to ask Jesus of whom xe spoke. The one lying on Jesus' breast asked xer, Boss, who is it? Jesus answered, It's the one to whom I give this bread after soaking it. When xe had soaked it, xe gave it to Judas, son of Simon the Iscariot. As soon as he received the bread, the satan entered him. Jesus told him, What you are going to do, do quickly. No one reclining at the table knew why xe said this to him. Some of them thought, because Judas kept the shared purse, that Jesus was telling him, Go to the town square and buy what we need for the feast, or, Give something to the poor. Accepting the bread, he left immediately. It was night.

When he'd left, Jesus said, Now the xon of humanity is glorified, and the god glorified in xer. And the god will glorify xer in xerself, and glorify xer immediately. Children, I am with you only a moment longer. You will seek me, but (as I told the Jews, so I tell you) where I am going, you cannot come. I give you a new commandment, that you love one another. As I have loved you, love one another. By this all will know that you are my apprentices, if you have love for one another.

Don't disturb your hearts; believe in the god and believe in me. In my fother's house there are many rooms; if there weren't, would I have told you that I go to prepare a place for you? And if I go to prepare a place for you, I will come again and gather you to myself, so that you can be where I am. And you know the way to where I'm going. Thomas said to xer, Boss, we don't know where you're going; how could we know the way? Jesus told him, I am the way and the truth and the life; no one comes to the fother except through me. If you know me, you will also know my fother, and from now on you will know xer and see xer. Philip said to xer, Boss, show us the fother, and it will suffice for us. Jesus said to him, All this time I've been with you, and you still don't know me,

Philip? One who sees me sees the fother. How can you say, Show us the fother? Don't you believe that I am in the fother and the fother is in me? The words I tell you, I don't say on my own, but the fother who inhabits me performs the works. Believe me, that I am in the fother and the fother is in me; if not, believe because of the works. Truly, truly I tell you, the one who believes on me will do the same works I do, and will do even greater works, because I am going to the fother. And whatever you ask in my name, I will do, so that the fother will be glorified in the xon. If you ask me for anything in my name, I will do it.

If you love me, you will keep my commandments. I will ask the fother, and xe will give you another helper to be with you forever, the breath of truth, that the world cannot receive, because it neither sees it nor knows it. But you know it, because it stays with you and will be in you. I will not leave you orphaned; I will come to you. In a little while the world will no longer see me, but you will see me. Because I live, you will live. On that day you will know that I am in the fother and you in me and I in you. The one who has my commandments and keeps them is the one who loves me; the one who loves me will be loved by my fother, and I will love that one and reveal myself to that one. Judas, not Iscariot, asked xer, Boss, how will you reveal yourself to us and not to the world? In answer Jesus told him, The one who loves me will keep my word, and my fother will love that one, and we will come to that one and make our home with that one. One who does not love me does not kccp my words; the word you hear is not mine, but that of the fother who sent me.

All these things I've said to you while I've stayed with you. But the helper, the holy breath, that the fother sends in my name, will teach you everything and remind you of everything I've said to you. I charge you with peace, I give you my peace. I don't give to you the way the world gives. Don't be troubled at heart, or anxious. You heard me tell you, I go away but I'll come back to you. If you loved me, you would be glad for me that I go to the fother, because the fother is greater than I am. tell you this now, before it happens, so that when it happens you'll believe. From now on I won't say much to you, because the principal of the world is coming. He has nothing on me, but so that the world will know I love the fother, I do as the fother has instructed me. Get up; let's go.

I am the true vine, and my father the farmer. Every branch on me that bears no fruit xe prunes, and every branch that does bear fruit xe trims so that it will bear even more fruit. You are trim through the word I have spoken to you. You remain in me, and I in you. The branch can't bear fruit by itself, detached from the vine, and neither can you, detached from me. I am the vine; you are the branches. The one who remains in me and I in that one bears much fruit, though detached from me that one could do nothing. Those who do not remain in me, I cut off like a branch, and they dry up, and are gathered and tossed onto the fire and burned. If you remain in me and my sayings remain in you, ask what you will and it will be done for you. In this is my fother glorified, that you bear much fruit and become my apprentices. As the fother loves me, I love you; remain in my love. If you keep my commandments, you will remain in my love, as I, keeping my fother's commandments, remain in xer love.

I've told you these things so that my joy may be in you, and your joy be full. This is my commandment, that you love one another as I have loved you. No one has greater love than this, to forfeit one's soul to one's friends. You are my friends if you do what I have commanded you to. From now on I don't call you slaves, because the slave doesn't know what the boss does; I call you friends, because I've made known to you all that I've heard from my fother. You didn't choose me; I chose you and charged you to bear fruit that will keep, so that what you ask of the fother in my name xe will give you. This I command you: love one another.

If the world hates you, know that it hated me before it hated you. If you belonged to the world, the world would love you, its own, but because you don't belong to the world, because I have chosen you, the world hates you. Remember the word I told you, The slave is not greater than the boss. If they persecuted me, they'll persecute you; if they kept my word, they'll keep yours. All these things they'll do to you against my name, because they don't know the one who sent me. If I hadn't come and spoken to them, they would have no error, but now they have no excuse for their errors. One who hates me also hates my fother. If I hadn't done among them works no one else did, they would have no error, but now they have seen and hated both me and my fother. This fulfills the word written in their law, *They hated me without cause.*

When the helper has come, whom I will send you from the fother, the breath of truth that comes from the fother, xe will attest to me. And you must attest, because you have been with me from the beginning.

I've told you these things so you won't stumble. They'll kick you out of the synagogues; indeed, an hour is coming when those who kill you will think they give service to the god. They'll do these things to you because they have not known the fother or me. But I've told you these things so that when the hour for them comes you will remember that I warned you of them.

I didn't tell you these things from the beginning, because I was with you. But now I am going to the one who sent me, and none of you has asked, Where are you going? But because I've told you these things, sorrow has filled your hearts. But I tell you the truth, it's better for you that I go, because until I go the helper will not come to you, but if I go I'll send it to you. Its coming will convince the world about error and justice and judgment: error, because they don't believe in me; justice, because I am going to the fother and you will no longer see me; judgment, because the principal of the world has been judged.

I have much more to tell you, but you can't bear it now. When it comes, the breath of truth, it will guide you to all truth. It will not speak on its own, but will say what it hears, and will report to you what is to come. It will glorify me by receiving from me and reporting to you. Everything the fother has is mine; that's why I say it will receive from me and report to you.

A little while, and you won't see me; another little while, and you'll see me. Some of xer apprentices wondered to one another, Why does xe say to us, A little while, and you won't see me; another little while, and you'll see me? and, Because I am going to the fother? They asked, What is this "little while"? We don't know what xe's saying. Jesus knew they wanted to ask xer, so xe said to them, Are you asking one another what I meant when I said, A little while, and you won't see me; another little while, and you'll see me? Truly, truly I tell you, you will weep and lament, but the world will rejoice; you will suffer, but your suffering will become joy. A woman in labor suffers because her hour has come, but once she has given birth to her child, she no longer remembers the pain, because of the joy of having brought a human into the world. Now you have suffering, but I will see you again, and your heart will rejoice, and no one will take your joy from you. On that day you'll no longer ask me anything. Truly, truly I tell you, if you ask anything of the fother in my name, xe will give it to you. Up to now, you haven't asked for anything in my name; but ask and you will receive, so that your joy will be complete.

I've said these things to you in figures; an hour is coming when I will no longer speak to you in figures, but plainly report to you about the fother. On that day you will ask in my name, and I will not speak for you to the fother, because the fother xerself loves you, because you loved me and believed that I came from the god. I came from the fother and have come into the world; now I am leaving the world and going back to the fother. Xer apprentices said, Look, now you are saying things plainly, speaking without figures. Now we know that you know everything, and that no one need question you. By this we believe that you have come from god. Jesus answered them, Now you believe? Look, the hour comes, has come already, when you will scatter, each to his own home, leaving me alone, but I am not alone, because the fother is with me. I've said these things to you so that in me you may have peace. In the world you have troubles, but have courage: I have conquered the world.

Having said these things, Jesus raised xer eyes to the sky and said, Fother, the hour has come; glorify your xon, so that the xon may glorify you, just as you have given xer authority over all flesh, to give timeless life to all you have given xer. This timeless life is so that they may know you, the only true god, and the one you sent, Jesus the salve. I have glorified you on earth by completing the work you gave me to do. So now glorify me, fother, with you, with the glory I had with you before the world began.

I revealed your name to the humans you gave me from the world. They were yours and you gave them to me, and they have kept their word. Now they know that everything you gave me is from you, because the sayings you gave me I gave to them, and they received them and know truly that I came from you, and they believe that you sent me. I ask on their behalf. I don't ask on behalf of the world, but on behalf of those you've given me, because they are yours. All of mine are yours, and yours mine, and I am glorified in them. I am no longer in the world, but they are in the world, and I am coming to you. Holy fother, keep in your name those you have given me, so that they be one as we are one. While I was with them, I kept in your name those you gave me. I guarded them, and none was lost except the son of waste, so that the writing be fulfilled. But now I am coming to you. I speak these things in the world so they may have my joy, fulfilled in themselves. I gave them your word and the world hated them because they are not of the world, just as I am not of the world. I don't ask that you take them out of the world, but that you keep them from the harmful one. They are not of the world, just as I am not of the world. Consecrate them with the truth: your word is truth. As you sent me into the world, so I sent them into the world. For them I consecrate myself, so that they be consecrated in truth.

I ask not for them only, but also for those who believe in me through their word, so that all may be one, as you, fother, are in me and I in you, so that the world may believe that you sent me. And the glory you gave me I gave them, that they be one as we are one, me in them and you in me, that they be perfected as one, that the world know you sent me, and that you love them as you love me. Fother, those given me, I will that where I am they may be with me, to look on my glory, which you gave me because you loved me before the foundation of the world. Just fother, the world does not know you, but I know you, and they know you sent me. I made known to them your name, so that the love with which you loved me may be in them, and I be in them.

They went to a place with the name Gethsemane, and xe told xer apprentices, Sit here while I pray. Xe took Peter and James and John with xer, and began to be troubled and dispirited, and said to them, My soul is sorrowed to death. Remain here and keep watch. Going a little farther, xe fell to the ground and prayed that if possible the hour pass xer by. Xe said, Abba the fother, anything is possible for you; take away this cup from me. But do your will, not mine. Xe came and found them sleeping, and said to Peter, Simon, you're sleeping? You couldn't keep watch for one hour? Watch and pray that you not come to trial. The breath is eager but the flesh is feeble. Again xe went off and prayed, saying the same words. And again xe came and found them sleeping, because their eyes were heavy, and they didn't know how to answer xer. Xe came a third time and said to them, Still sleeping and taking rest. Enough. Look, the xon of humanity is betrayed into the hands of errants. Get up, let's go. Look, my betrayer's here.

Immediately, even as xe spoke, Judas arrived, one of the twelve, and with him a crowd of chief priests and scribes and elders, with swords and clubs. The betrayer had arranged with them a signal, saying, The one I kiss is xer; seize xer, and take xer away securely. He came, and came up to her, and said, Rabbi, and kissed xer. They laid their hands on xer and seized xer. One of the bystanders drew his sword and struck the high priest's slave and cut off his ear. But in answer Jesus said to them, As if against a robber, have you come out with swords and clubs to take hold of me? Every day I was with you in the temple teaching, and you didn't seize me; but the writings must be fulfilled. And everyone deserted xer and fled.

A young man was following xer wearing only a linen drape over his nakedness, and they seized him. But he left behind the drape, and fled naked.

They brought Jesus before the high priest, and all the chief priests and elders and scribes gathered. Peter followed xer at a distance, right into the courtyard of the high priest, and sat with the guards, warming himself at the fire. The chief priests and the whole council were seeking testimony against Jesus, to put xer to death, but found none. Many testified falsely against xer, but their testimony didn't agree. Some stood up and testified falsely against xer, saying, We heard xer saying, , I will destroy this sanctuary that is made with hands, and in three days build another one not made with hands. But none of their testimonies matched. The chief priest stood front and center and questioned Jesus, saying, You have no answer to these testimonies against you? But xe stayed silent and didn't answer. Again the chief priest questioned xer and said to xer, Are you the salve, the xon of the blessed one? Jesus said, I am,

and you will see the xon of humanity

sitting to the right of the powerful one,

and coming with the clouds of the sky.

The chief priest tore his clothes and said, Why would we need more witnesses? You heard the blasphemy: how does it look to you? They all condemned xer, as deserving death. Some began to spit on xer. They covered xer face and hit xer and said to xer, Prophesy. And the guards received xer with blows to the head. While Peter was below in the courtyard, one of the chief priest's slavegirls came by, and seeing Peter warming himself she looked intently at him and said, You were with Jesus of Nazareth. He denied it, saying, I don't know you or understand what you're saying. And he went out into the forecourt, just as the cock crowed. The slavegirl who'd seen him said again, this time to some bystanders, This is one of them. Again he denied it. A little later the bystanders said to Peter, Surely you're one of them; you're a Galilean. He began to curse and swear, I don't know the one you're talking about. And immediately the cock crowed a second time, and Peter remembered the word Jesus had said to him, Before the cock crows twice you will disavow me three times. And he broke down and wept.

Early in the morning the chief priests held a meeting with the elders and the scribes and the whole council, and they bound Jesus and led xer away and delivered xer to Pilate.

Then Judas, who had betrayed xer, seeing that xe was condemned, remorsefully returned the thirty silvers to the chief priests and elders, saying, I have erred in betraying innocent blood. They said, What's that to us? See to that yourself. He threw down the silvers into the sanctuary, and went away and hanged himself. The chief priests picked up the silvers and said, It wouldn't be lawful to put this into the treasury, since it's blood money. After conferring, they used the silvers to buy the potter's field as a burial ground for foreigners, which is why to this day that field is called the Field of Blood. This fulfilled what had been said by the prophet Jeremiah, *And they took thirty silvers, the price at which the priceless was priced by the sons of Israel, and gave them for the potter's field, by order of the boss.*

The governor's standard bearers were holding up the standards, and when Jesus entered, the pinnacles of the standards bowed and worshiped Jesus. When the Jews saw the images on the standards, how they bowed and worshiped Jesus, they complained loudly about the standard bearers. Pilate asked the Jews, Aren't you amazed at how the pinnacles bowed and worshiped Jesus? The Jews said to Pilate, We saw how the standard bearers bowed and worshiped xer. The governor called the standard bearers forward and asked them, Why did you do this? They said to Pilate, We are Greek men, temple slaves. How could we worship xer? While we were holding them up, the images themselves bowed down and worshiped xer.

Pilate told the synagogue leaders and the elders of the people, Choose for yourselves strong and sturdy men, and have them hold up the standards: we'll see if they bow on their own. The elders of the Jews assigned twelve sturdy and strong men, six to hold up each standard, and stood them before the governor's seat. Pilate told the courier, Lead xer out of the Praetorium, then bring xer in again in whatever way you like. Jesus and the courier went out of the Praetorium. Pilate called forward the ones who'd held the images before, and said to them, I swear by the preservation of Caesar, if the standards don't bow when Jesus enters, I'll cut off your heads. The governor ordered Jesus to enter a second time. When xe entered, again the standards bowed and worshiped xer.

Jesus stood before the governor, and the governor questioned xer, saying, Are you the king of the Jews? Jesus said, If you say so. And to the accusations of the chief priests and elders, xe did not reply. Then Pilate said to xer, Don't you hear how many accusations they make against you? And xe answered with not a single word, to the amazement of the governor.

At that festival the governor customarily released for the crowd the prisoner of their choice, and had at that point a notorious prisoner named Barabbas. So when the crowd had gathered, Pilate asked, Which do you want me to release, Barabbas or Jesus who is called the salve? He saw that it had been from envy that they had handed xer over. While he was still at the bench, his wife sent him this message, Have nothing to do with this just person; I suffered much today from a dream about xer. But the chief priests and elders persuaded the crowd to have Barabbas released and Jesus executed. Persisting, the governor asked them, Which do you want me to release to you? They said, Barabbas. Pilate asked them, What should I do with Jesus who is called the salve? They all said, Crucify xer. He asked, What has xe done wrong? But they shouted louder, Crucify xer. He asked, What has xe done wrong? But they shouted louder, Crucify xer. When Pilate saw he was getting nowhere, but that a riot was starting, he took water and washed his hands in front of the crowd, saying, I am innocent of this person's blood; see to it yourselves. Then in answer all the people said, Xer blood be on us and on our children. Then he released Barabbas to them, and after flogging Jesus, he handed xer over to be crucified.

╬

Then the soldiers of the governor took Jesus into the Praetorium and the whole platoon crowded around xer. They stripped xer and put a scarlet robe on xer. They twisted some thorns into a crown and set it on xer head, put a staff into xer right hand, and knelt before xer and mocked xer, saying, Hail, king of the Jews, and spit on xer and took the staff and hit xer over the head with it. After mocking xer, they stripped off the robe and put xer own clothes back on xer, and led xer out to crucify xer.

They made a passerby, Simon the Cyrenian, father of Alexander and Rufus, who had come in from the country, carry xer cross. And they brought xer to the place Golgotha, which translates as Skull Site. They gave xer myrrh-laced wine, but xe didn't take it. They crucified xer,

and divided xer clothes among themselves,

tossing lots to determine who got what.

It was midmorning when they crucified xer. The inscription of the charge against xer read, The King of the Jews. And with xer they crucified two thieves, one to xer right and one to xer left. Those who passed by xer taunted xer, shaking their heads and saying,

You who'll destroy the temple and rebuild it in three days, preserve yourself and come down from the cross. Similarly, the chief priests and scribes mocked xer among themselves, saying, Xe preserved others, but can't preserve xerself. Let the salve the king of Israel come down now from the cross, so we can see and believe. Even the ones being crucified with xer taunted xer.

Around noon, darkness covered the land until midafternoon. At midafternoon, Jesus cried out in a loud voice, *Eloi, Eloi, lama sabachthini?*, which translates as *My god, my god, why have you abandoned me?* Some of the bystanders, hearing xer, said, Listen, xe's calling for Elijah. One of them ran and soaked a sponge with sour wine and gave it to xer to drink, saying, Hang on, let's see if Elijah comes to take xer down. But Jesus cried out with a loud voice and breathed xer last breath. And the sanctuary curtain was torn in two from top to bottom. The centurion who stood facing xer, seeing xer breathe xer last breath, said, Truly this person was the xon of god. Also there were women watching from a distance, among them Mary Magdalene, Mary the mother of little James and Joses, and Salome. These women had followed xer and tended xer when xe was in Galilee, and many other women had come up with xer to Jerusalem.

When xe was crucified, darkness covered the whole earth. The sun was completely hidden and the dome was darkened during the day, so that the stars appeared, and the darkness had their glittering, as I'm sure you know, since people the world over lit lanterns from noon to night. The moon was like blood, and never shone the whole night, even though it was full. The stars of Orion mourned.

The sun of the power of the principals set, darkness overtook them, and the world gave way to its weakness. They bound xer with many bonds and nailed xer to the cross with four bronze nails, but xe tore the temple veil with xer own hands. An earth-quake released earth's chaos, and the souls that had been in the undersleep arose. They wandered openly, having taken off jealousy and ignorance, leaving them there beside the dead tombs, having put on the new person, and having come to know the graceful, whole one of the timeless, incomprehensible fother of infinite light, destroyer of the power of the principals.

Then on the sabbath, in the middle of the night the sun appeared, shining brighter than ever, and the whole sky was brightened. Like lightning striking in winter, some men dressed in sublime clothes of indescribable glory appeared in the air, and countless emissaries cried out and said, Glory to the highest god, and to earth the peace of people of good will. Get up from Hades, you who have been enslaved in the underworld of Hades. At their voice, all the mountains and hills quaked, and rocks split and great chasms opened in the earth, revealing the abyss.

In that fear the dead appeared standing up, as the Jews themselves observed, saying, We saw Abraham, Isaac, Jacob, and the twelve patriarchs, who dies more than two thousand five hundred years ago, and we clearly saw Noah in his body. And all those many walked around and with a loud voice sang a hymn to the god, saying, The one who stood up from the dead, our boss the god, has restored to life all the dead, and by plundering Hades has killed death.

That whole night, the light did not dim.

At evening, because it was preparation day, the day before the sabbath, Joseph of Arimathea, a prominent council member, who himself was watching for the realm of the god, boldly went to Pilate and asked for the body of Jesus. Pilate, surprised that xe was already dead, summoned a centurion and asked if xe had died. After confirmation from the centurion, Pilate gave the body to Joseph. He bought a linen cloth, took down the body, wrapped it in the linen cloth, and laid it in a tomb carved into the rock, and rolled a stone against the entrance of the tomb. Mary Magdalene and Mary the mother of Joses saw where xe was laid.

The next day, the one after the day of preparation, the chief priests and the Pharisees went together to Pilate, saying, Boss, we remember the deceiver saying while xe was alive, After three days I will stand up. Order that the tomb be secured through the third day, so that xer apprentices don't come and steal xer and say to the people, xe has risen from the dead, and the last deception prove worse than the first. Pilate said to them, You have your guard; go and set it as you see fit. So they went and secured the tomb, sealing the stone and setting the guard.

When the sabbath was over, Mary Magdalene, Mary the mother of Jesus, and Salome bought spices, so they could come and anoint xer. Very early on the first day after the sabbath, they came to the tomb soon after sunrise.

And look, there was a big earthquake, because an emissary of the boss came down from the sky and approached and rolled back the stone and sat on it, looking like lightning, wearing snow-white clothes. From fear, the guards trembled and became like corpses. In response, the emissary said to the women, Don't fear. I know you seek the crucified Jesus. Xe's not here; xe's gotten up, just like xe said. Come look at the place where xe was lain. Then go on quickly and tell xer apprentices that xe has gotten up from among the dead, and look, xe goes ahead of you to Galilee, where you will see xer. Look, I've told you. So they went on quickly from the tomb with fear and great joy, and ran to report this to xer apprentices. But look, Jesus met them, giving greeting. They approached and clasped xer feet and worshiped xer. Jesus said to them, Don't fear. Go and report to my siblings that they should go to Galilee; there they'll see me.

To say the boss first died and then stood up is imprecise: xe stood up first, before dying. People who say they themselves will die first and then stand up are mistaken: one who does not stand up first, before dying, will not stand up after.

And look, two of them on that same day were going to a village named Emmaus, seven miles from Jerusalem, talking together about all these things that had occurred. It happened while they were talking, conversing with one another, that Jesus xerself approached and went with them, but their eyes were kept from recognizing xer. Xe asked them, What words have you been exchanging with one another as you walk? They stood still, sad-faced. In reply, the one named Cleopas said to xer, Are you the only visitor to Jerusalem who doesn't know the things that have happened these days? Xe asked them, What things? They said to xer, Things about Jesus, who was a prophet strong in work and word before the god and all the people, how our chief priests and principals handed xer over to a death sentence and crucified xer. We were hoping xe would be the one to redeem Israel, and on top of all this it's the third day since these things happened, and some women from our group amazed us. They were at the tomb early, and didn't find xer body, and came saying they'd seen a vision of emissaries, who said xe's alive. Some who were with us went to the tomb and found it was just as the women had said: they didn't see xer. Xe said to them, O ignorant ones, slow of heart to believe all that the prophets spoke: shouldn't the salve have suffered these things and entered into xer glory? And starting with Moses xe explained to them all the prophets and all the writings concerning xer.

They neared the village where they were going, and xe made as if to go farther, but they urged xer, saying, Stay with us: it's toward evening, the day is almost over. And xe went in and stayed with them. It happened as xe reclined with them at table that xe took bread and blessed it and gave it to them. Their eyes were opened and they recognized xer, but xe disappeared from their sight. They said to each other, Weren't our hearts burning in us as xe talked with tus on the way, opening the writings to us? So they stood up at that moment and returned to Jerusalem and found the eleven gathered together, and others with them, saying, The boss actually got up, and has appeared to Simon. So the two recounted what had happened on their way and how they'd known it was xer as soon as xe broke the bread.

While they were still talking about xer, xe xerself stood among them and said to them, Peace to you. They were startled and fearful, thinking they were seeing a breath. But xe said to them, Why are you disturbed, and why do such thoughts rise up in your hearts? Look at my hands and feet, and see that it's me. Touch me and see, because breath does not have flesh and bones like I have, as you can see. Having said this, xe showed them xer hands and feet. They could hardly believe it, for joy and surprise, so xe asked them, Do you have any food to eat? They gave xer a piece of broiled fish, and xe took it and ate it in front of them.

Xe said to them, These are the words I said to you while I was with you, that everything written about me in the law of Moses and

and the prophets and the psalms must be fulfilled. Then xe opened their minds to understand the writings. And told them, It's written this way, for the salve to suffer, and stand up on the third day, and that reconsideration and release from errors be declared to all others, beginning in Jerusalem. You are witnesses of these things. Look, I deliver this promise from my fother to you, but stay in the city until you are clothed with power from above.

Thomas, one of the twelve, the one called the Twin, wasn't with them when Jesus came. The other apprentices told him, We've seen the boss. He said to them, Unless I see on his hands the wounds from the nails and put my fingers into those wounds and my hand into xer side, I won't believe. A week later, the apprentices again were indoors, and Thomas was with them. Though the doors were locked, Jesus came and stood among them and said, Peace to you. Then xe said to Thomas, Put your finger here and see my hands; reach out your hand and put it into my side. Don't be unbelieving but believing. In answer Thomas said to xer, My boss and my god. Jesus said to him, Because you've seen, you've come to believe me? Graceful are those who do not see, but still believe.

On the next day, the day of preparation, the synagogue leaders and the priests and the Levites rose and went to the house of Nicodemus. Nicodemus greeted them and said, Peace to you. They said, Peace to you and to Joseph, and to all your house and all the house of Joseph. He invited them into his house. The whole council sat, and Joseph sat between Annas and Caiaphas. No one said the first word to him, so Joseph asked, Why have you summoned me? They directed Nicodemus to speak to Joseph. Opening his mouth, Nicodemus said to Joseph, Father, you see that these honored teachers and priests and Levites seek to learn a bit from you. Joseph said, Ask. Taking up the law, Annas and Caiaphas placed Joseph under oath, saying, Give glory to the god of Israel, and give xer full confession. When Achar was placed under oath by the prophet Joshua, he did not perjure himself, but reported everything to him, concealing nothing. Now you conceal nothing from us. Joseph said, I'll conceal not one word. They said to him, We were quite hurt that you asked for the body of Jesus and wrapped it in clean linen and laid it in a tomb. That's why we closed you in a windowless house, and locked and sealed the door, and posted guards to watch where you were closed in. When we opened it on the sabbath and didn't find you, we were hurt. All the people of the boss have been perplexed to this point. Now report to us what happened.

Joseph said, On the day of preparation, late afternoon, you locked me in and I stayed the whole sabbath. In the middle of the night, while I stood praying, the house I was locked in was lifted up by its four corners, and I saw a flash of lightning with my own eyes. I was filled with fear and fell to the ground. Someone took me by the hand and picked me up from the place I had fallen. A wet dew shrouded me, head to foot, and a scent of myrrh entered my nose. Xe wiped my face, kissed me, and said to me, Don't fear, Joseph. Open your eyes and see who is talking with you. Looking up, I saw Jesus. I trembled, and started thinking it was a ghost, so I said the commandments. But xe kept speaking to me, and as you know about a ghost, if it meets someone and hears the commandments, it flees immediately. So, seeing that xe kept speaking to me, I said to xer, Rabbi Elijah. Xe said to me, I am not Elijah. So I asked xer, Who are you, boss? Xe told me, I am Jesus, whose body you requested from Pilate. You wrapped me in clean linen and placed a cloth over my face, and laid me in your new cave, and rolled a huge stone in front of the entrance to the cave. I said to the one speaking to me, Show me the place where I laid you. Xe led me out and showed me the place where I'd laid xer, and the linen lay there, and the cloth that had been over xer face. Then I knew it was Jesus. Xe took my hand, and stood me back in my house, with the doors still locked. Xe led me to my bed and said to me, Peace to you. Xe kissed me and told me, For forty days, don't leave your house. Look, I'm going to my siblings in Galilee.

After these things Jesus showed xerself to the apprentices again by the Sea of Tiberias. There together were Simon Peter, Thomas called the Twin, Nathanael from Cana in Galilee, the sons of Zebedee, and two others of xer apprentices. Simon Peter said to them, I'm going fishing. They said to him, We'll come with you. They immediately went and boarded a boat, but caught nothing that night. At daybreak Jesus stood at the shore, but the apprentices didn't recognize that it was Jesus. Jesus said to them, Kids, have anything to eat? They replied to xer, No. Xe told them, Cast your net over the right side of the boat and you'll find something. They cast, and could not haul in the net, it was so full of fish. The apprentice Jesus loved said to Peter, It's the boss. When Simon Peter heard it was the boss, he grabbed his clothes (he'd been naked) and dove into the sea. The other apprentices came in the boat, which hadn't been far from shore, dragging the net full of fish. When they got out on shore, they saw a charcoal fire with fish on it, and bread. Jesus told them, Bring some of those fingerlings you've caught. Simon Peter went over and hauled the net ashore full of large fish, a hundred and fifty-three of them, and even though there were so many, the net was not torn. Jesus invited them, Come, have breakfast. The apprentices didn't dare ask xer, Who are you?, knowing it was the boss. Jesus came and took the bread and gave it to them, and the same with the fish. This was now the third time Jesus showed xerself to the apprentices after getting up from the dead.

After they'd breakfasted, Jesus said to Simon Peter, Simon, son of John, do you love me more than these do? He said to xer, Yes, boss, you know I love you. Xe told him, Tend my lambs. Xe asked him again, a second time, Simon, son of John, do you love me? He said to xer, Yes, boss, you know I love you. Xe told him, Shepherd my flocks. Xe asked him a third time, Simon, son of John, do you love me? Peter was troubled that xe'd asked him a third time, Do you love me?, and said to xer, Boss, you know everything, you know I love you. Xe told him, Tend my flocks. Truly, truly I tell you, when you were young, you could dress yourself and go where you wanted; once you're old, you'll stretch out your hands and someone else will dress you and lead where you don't want to go. Xe said this to indicate the kind of death by which xe would glorify the god, and having said this, xe told him, Follow me.

The apprentices asked, When that time comes, will matter melt away or not? The preserver said, Natures and structures and creatures all exist with one another, through one another. Everything will be absorbed ultimately into its own roots, because the nature of matter absorbs its natural rootedness. Anyone with ears to hear, hear.

Peter said, Since you've explained all else to us, also tell us this: What is the error of the world? The preserver said, Error does not *exist*. Instead, you *perform* error when you imitate the nature of the faithlessness called error. Against this, the good inhabits you, restoring each nature to its nature, to its roots. Continuing, xe said, That is why you fall ill and die. Whoever has understanding, understand.

Matter imposes energy, the against-nature that charges all bodies. That's why I told you, Be receptive. Even if you are not well-received, still be receptive to the diversity of forms in nature. Anyone with ears to hear, hear.

After saying this, the graceful blessed them all, saying, Peace be with you. Receive to yourselves my peace. Take care that no one leads you astray, saying Look over here or Look over there. The xon of humanity is within you. Follow xer. Those who seek xer find xer. Go then, and proclaim the good news of the realm. Do not make any rules beyond what I have set for you, and do not make law as if you were the lawgiver, or you will be bound to it.

After saying this, xe left. They were upset, and wept loudly, asking, How can we go to others and proclaim the good news of the realm of the xon of humanity? If they didn't spare xer, why think they'll spare us? Then Mary stood and blessed them all, instructing her brothers, Don't weep. Don't be upset or irresolute: xer grace will inhabit you and protect you. Instead, let's praise xer greatness, xe who prepares us and humanizes us. By saying this, Mary turned their hearts toward the good, and they began to exercise the words of the preserver.

Peter said to Mary, Sister, we know the preserver loved you more than the other women. Tell us what you remember of the words of the preserver, the ones only you know, that we have not heard. Mary answered, saying, What was withheld from you I will tell you. And she began speaking these words to them: I saw the boss in a vision. I said, Boss, today I saw you in a vision. Xe replied, saying to me, I bless you because you did not shy away from facing me. Value attends disposition. I asked xer, Boss, how does one who sees a vision see it, with soul or with breath? The preserver replied, saying, One sees neither with soul nor with breath; mind, which is between them, is what sees the vision.

Mary recounted to the others the whole of her vision, which ended at the manifestations of anger: The first, she said, is darkness.

The second is desire, the third ignorance, the fourth the death drive, the fifth tyranny of the flesh, the sixth self-deception by the flesh, the seventh righteous indignation. These, the seven manifestations of anger, asked the soul, Where have you come from, murderer of humans, and where are you going, pillager of space? The soul, in answer, said, What ruled me has been assassinated, what besieged me has been defeated. My desire has atrophied and my ignorance has died. I was freed from one world by another world, from one example by a higher example. The fleeting hold of forgetfulness released me into the suspension of time and season and age by silence.

After saying this, Mary fell silent, since this ended what the preserver had said to her. Andrew spoke up, saying to the brothers, Think what you want about what was just said, but I for one do not believe the preserver said this; these teachings don't sound at all familiar. Peter, too, objected, asking the others about the preserver: Would xe speak with a woman alone, without also telling us? Should we turn away from xer toward her? Did xe prefer her to us?

Mary, weeping, addressed Peter: Peter, my brother, what do you think? Do you think I've made this up by myself and am lying about the preserver? Levi responded to Peter, saying, Peter, you've always been rash. Now you are contesting her as our adversaries do, but if the preserver found her worthy who are you to reject her? Surely the preserver knows her well enough. Not without reason did xe love her more than xe loved us. Let's be humble, complete in our humanity, presenting ourselves according to xer instruction, proclaiming the good news, laying down no rule beyond what the preserver gave us.

When Levi had said this, they went out to proclaim and teach.

The twelve apprentices were sitting together, recalling to one another what the preserver had said to each, whether openly or in secret, and organizing it into books. And look, the preserver appeared to them, five hundred and fifty days after xe rose from the dead. Xe said, Leave James and Peter to me. Xe took them aside, and told the rest to keep doing what they'd been doing.

Jesus challenged them, How dare you spare the flesh, you for whom the breath is a protecting wall? Only consider how long the world existed before you and will exist after you, to see that your life is a day and your sufferings an hour. Be seekers of death: when you ask after death, it will teach you about being chosen. Truly I tell you, no one who fears death will be preserved.

Again I warn you, you who are, be like those who are not, so you may dwell among those who are not. Don't make the realm of the sky into a desert in you. Don't be proud of the illuminating light, but act toward one another as I have acted toward you. I placed myself under a curse for you, so you could be preserved. That's all I'll tell you for now. For now, I return to the place from which I came.

Having said these words, xe departed.

╬

After xe rose from the dead, xer twelve male and seven female apprentices continued to be xer followers. They went to Galilee, to the hill called Prophecy and Joy. They gathered together, in perplexity about the true nature of the universe, the plan of salvation, divine providence, the power of the principals, and what the preserver intended for them in the secret workings of holiness. The preserver was present, not in xer prior form, but intangible as breath, bright as an emissary of light, in a form I can't presume to describe. Mortal flesh could not bear it, only flesh clean and complete, like xe taught about on the Mount of Olives in Galilee.

Xe greeted them, Peace be with you, my peace I give to you. They were amazed and afraid, but the preserver, laughing, offered, What are you mulling over? Why such perplexity? What are you still wondering about?

Philip said, The true nature of the universe.

The preserver said to them, I'll have you know that all humans born on earth from the creation of the world to now are dust, so, ask as they will about who the god is and the god is like, have not found out. The wisest among them have speculated on the basis of the order of the cosmos and the movements of its parts, but such speculations miss the truth. But I, who come from infinite light, am the truth, and give you to know the truth.

The graceful preserver said this, then disappeared from them. The apprentices continued in the joy of the breath from that day on, proclaiming the good news from the god, the timeless, imperishable breath.

The apprentices gathered again, and Jesus, appearing among them, said to them, Peace be with you, and with all who honor my name. When you go, you go with joy and grace and power. Don't be afraid. I am with you forever. These signs will attend those who believe: in my name they will expel visitants, they'll speak with new tongues, they'll pick up snakes in their hands, and if they drink anything deadly it won't hurt them, and they'll lay their hands on the sick, who'll recover.

Why fret? Why fear? Don't be fainthearted. I am with you always. I am fother, mather, child. I am the uncorrupted and incorruptible one, come to teach you what is and was and will be, so you may apprehend the invisible with the visible; to teach you maturation into perfect humanity. Turn your face upward, to hear the things I tell you now, so you can convey to others who, sharing your breath, would mature into perfect humans. Be courageous. Fear nothing. I am with you. I am nearer you than the clothes on your body.

Then, when boss Jesus had spoken with them, xe was taken up into the sky and xe sat down at the right hand of the god. They went out declaring this everywhere, the boss working with them and confirming the word with the attending signs.

Jesus worked many other wonders, but were they written one by one, I doubt the very cosmos could contain the books thus written.

This is the knowledge of the living book revealed to the timeless realms in ultimacy, as letters not mere vowels and consonants in which one might read mere trivialities, but letters of truth that speak self-knowledge, each letter a complete truth, a complete book, the letters that write the unity of the fother for the timeless realms, so they may know the fother.

About the word: wisdom contemplates it, teaching speaks it, knowledge discloses it, patience crowns it, joy harmonizes with it, glory exalts it, image reveals it, rest receives it, love embodies it, trust embraces it.

We embrace the realm of the salve in order to abolish inequality, injustice, and discrimination, to return in the end to unity as we began in unity, without male and female, slave and free, circumcised and uncircumcised, citizen and alien, but all salved and salving. For the disenfranchised, rights; for the disadvantaged, empowerment.

Steady the feet of those who stumble and extend your hands to the sick. Feed the hungry, offer rest to the tired, help up those who want to stand, awaken those who sleep.

The god is here, not there. The harmful cannot harm you. Peace be with you.

Additional Reading

Many readers will have arrived at *The Gospel* having read a great deal already about the gospel, and the curious reader will have no trouble finding further reading: it is hard to think of any subject about which more has been written. Here I simply mention a very few of the sources on which I have drawn directly in composing *The Gospel*.

The Czeslaw Milosz poem, "Readings," quoted above, appears on page 262 of his *New and Collected Poems 1931-2001* (Ecco Press, 2003). Mieke Bal makes the distinction mentioned above in her book *Narratology* (Univ. of Toronto Press, 1997). The related distinction of mine is made in *Morte d'Author: An Autopsy* (Temple Univ. Press, 1990).

Various English translations of the four canonical Gospels are presented side-by-side in *The Precise Parallel New Testament*, edited by John R. Kohlenberger III (Oxford Univ. Press, 1995).

Three of the Biblical Gospels (those of Matthew, Mark, and Luke) share so much of their material that they have come to be called collectively the synoptic Gospels. Various "gospel parallels" have been constructed to compare the three. In composing *The Gospel*, I used *Gospel Parallels: A Synopsis of the First Three Gospels* (3rd edition), edited by Burton H. Throckmorton, Jr. (Thomas Nelson Inc., 1967).

No one book collects all of the existing "apocryphal" Gospels. Two important anthologies that contain multiple Gospels are: *The Apocryphal Gospels: Texts and Translations*, by Bart D. Ehrman and Zlatko Pleše (Oxford Univ. Press, 2011), and *The Coptic Gnostic Library: A Complete Edition of the Nag Hammadi Codices*, edited by James M. Robinson (Brill, 2000).

In composing *The Gospel*, I drew also on a different type of anthology, one that presents selections rather than whole Gospels, William D. Stroker's *Extracanonical Sayings of Jesus* (Scholars Press, 1989). I also drew on volumes that present single Gospels, such as Christopher Tuckett's edition of *The Gospel of Mary* (Oxford Univ. Press, 2007), and *The Gospel of Judas: Critical Edition*, edited by Rudolphe Kasser and Gregor Wurst (National Geographic, 2007).

H. L. Hix's previous work includes a retelling of the Book of Job, as "A Manual of Happiness" in *First Fire, Then Birds*, and a redaction and translation of a sayings gospel, as "Near Fire" in *Rain Inscription*.